FEAR OF FRYING

I could imagint your smile when your read and laugh, keep your smile forever...

love you

To my Dad, who gave me a sense of humor, and to my Mom who helped me keep it when he passed away.

FEAR OF FRYING

AND OTHER FAX OF LIFE

✸

✸

✸

JOSH FREED

Véhicule Press

ACKNOWLEDGEMENTS

Thanks to the people who contribute to my weekly world. My in-house editor Ingrid Peritz adds her insight and humor to every story. My out-house editors Victor Dabby and Tom Puchniak, tell me when things *aren't* funny. Stephen Phizicky, Sheila Arnopoulos, Gerry Bergeron, Jon Kalina and my brother Mike Freed are there when I'm desperate. Thanks also to Marilyn Mill, Quinn McIlhone,and the other *Montreal Gazette* editors who keep me alive after my deadline.

Published with the assistance of The Canada Council.
Cover art and design: J.W. Stewart
Cover photograph of author: Thomas Leon Königsthal Jr.
Interior design and imaging: Simon Garamond
Printing: Imprimerie d'Édition Marquis Ltée
Special thanks to Abbey and Irene.

CANADIAN CATALOGUING IN PUBLICATION DATA

Freed, Josh, 1949-
  Fear of frying and other fax of life

A collection of stories from author's Gazette column

ISBN 1-55065-057-2

1. Canadian wit and humour (English). I. Title.

PN6178.C3F74 1994   C818'.5402   C94-900849-4

Published by Véhicule Press, P.O.B. 125, Place du Parc Station, Montréal, Québec.
Distributed in Canada by General Distribution Services, Don Mills, Ontario and Niagara Falls, N.Y.

Printed in Canada on acid-free paper.

Contents

INTRODUCTION 7

1. THE FAX OF LIFE

Sleepless in Montreal 11
Car Bazaar 14
Air Scare 17
Electronic Love 20
None of the Above 23
No English 26
North To Nowhere 29
Unintelligence Briefing 32
The Gull War: I.Battle on the Poop Deck 35

2. HEALTH SCARE

Rest in Grease 41
Junk Mail Memory 44
Hair Today ... 47
Take My Polls 50
Remain Calm!! 53
Born to Lose 56
A Tipple a Day 59
The Write Stuff 62

3. CITY BLIGHTS

Battle of the Bagel 67
Arctic Chair 70
Festival of the Shadfly 72
Learning le French 74
The Sex of Restaurants 77
Neverendum Referendum 78
The Hardwhere Store 81
Operation Winter Storm 83

4. THE U.S. AND US

The U.S. and Us (I) 86
The U.S. and Us (II) 89
The U.S. and Us (III) 92
Mad About Metric 95
How's your Constitution? 98
Constitutional Knock-Out 101
Common Law Country 104

Border Disorder 106
The Gull War: II. Return of Attila 109

5. AWAY IN L.A.

Why Not Worry 114
Alien Rights 117
Nervous Service 119
Say Hi or Die 121
Gavel-gazing 124
Hapless Holiday 127
As the Olympic World Turns 130
The World's Best Column 132

6. ANARCHY AND BUREAUCRACY (+GST)

H.R. Freed 137
Read At Your Own Risk 140
Secretly Me 146
Voice Jail 149
Don't Mess With My Mess 152
Better Late Forever 152
The Gull War: III. Victory at Balcony 155

Introduction

As the world becomes a less dangerous place for humans to inhabit, we discover more and more things to frighten us. Fear of flying in planes, fear of frying our food, fear of frying our skin in the now deadly sun.

We are scared of soft stomachs and hard arteries; killer computer viruses, killer popcorn and killer bees. In the nineties, the innocuous has become dangerous.

Our anxiety is understandable. A fast-changing world requires new kinds of people, and unfortunately, we are not them. We must know our height in centimetres, then convert to Celsius and add GST. We must eat, drink and be wary, because we face RISK OF CHOLESTEROL every time we open a bottle of ketchup.

Even being a Canadian has become frightening. For more than a century, we were a blessedly bland people who did not bother to learn the words to our national anthem. Today, we are the Woody Allen of nations, a neurotic country caught up in a never-ending adolescent identity crisis.

We must have our vital signs checked by constitutional committees and our polls taken every day. We are condemned to live in a political time warp with no apparent exit—The Curse of the Constitution. The Neverendum Referendum.

Our country works well in practice, but not in theory.

In the face of such adversity there is no place to take refuge but in humor. As a clever woman once said: "He who laughs, lasts." And for the sake of my health, I try to laugh at least once every week. This book is the result. The stories in it are an updated collection from a weekly Saturday column I write in the *Montreal Gazette*. People always ask me how I get my ideas, and I always credit the same inspiration:

Desperation.

As a disorganized person (see page 149), I can never think of a topic until the last moment (see page 152). Clarity often comes with fear. Other times, only fear comes (see page 17).

Frankly, my best ideas usually crystallize at the end of the writing day, several minutes after I've filed a story and it's too late to change it. Which is why I like to do collections like this one. It's one of those rare chances you have to go back and get something right.

The stories that follow range from the personal to the political. They poke fun at fat cats, bureaucrats, sign laws, snowstorms, HAZARDOUS WARNING labels, second-hand steak fumes, quiet Canadians, noisy Americans and other fax of Canadian life.

Also included is a series of stories I wrote during a recent six-month stay in Los Angeles—a place I highly recommend to bring out the Canadian in you.

Who am I and why should you trust me? I'm calligraphy-challenged, hair-impaired and directionally-disabled. My desk is a mess, my imparfait is imperfect and my voice mail feels more like voice jail. I suffer from fear of flying and fear of frying.

If I can smile, so can you.

CHAPTER ONE

The Fax of Life

Sleepless in Montreal

GOOD MORNING. Many of you probably spent last night doing something boring, like sleeping — but not me. I read books. I planned the guest list for my 1995 Halloween party. I counted odd numbers backwards starting from 10,000.

I did all this while I was trying to sleep, fighting off occasional insomnia I've suffered ever since I was old enough to climb out of a crib. I don't sleep when I'm too unhappy, or too happy. I don't sleep when I eat too late, or too early.

In truth, I haven't slept like a baby since I was one.

I have always envied you people who sleep well. You sleep lying down, sitting at your desk and standing in the bus. You sleep through fires, floods, earthquakes and bankruptcy.

"I don't know how I do it," you say, with a sleepy smile. "I just close my eyes and Zzzzzz—I'm asleep. In fact I'm having a hard time staying awake right now."

Fortunately, I'm not a full-time insomniac—one of those people with bags under their eyes deep enough to pack luggage in. I just stay up part-time, several times a month. I'll sleep like a log for 4½ hours, then wake up with my mind in high gear, eager to worry about everything from Boris Yeltsin's wheat shortage to the fact I forgot to floss.

Unfortunately, the middle of the night is the worst time to worry. Routine chores seem like Herculean tasks: picking a wedding present for someone is a life-and-death choice; an unpaid telephone bill of $17.56 leads directly to Bordeaux jail. At 4 a.m., I'm sure it will destroy my credit rating, cause Visa to cancel my credit card and the bank to repossess my house.

"I'll be homeless and searching the gutter for orange rinds. And then there's that unpaid parking ticket! Oh God, I could get the chair!"

Once my mind starts buzzing I am like the princess who couldn't sleep because there was a pea under her mattress. My blanket seems too thick and my blinds too thin, my sheets too prickly and my pillow too stiff. And why is the fridge humming so loudly?

Everything seems to conspire against my sleep. As Gilbert and Sullivan once wrote in a song about insomnia:

The bedding all creeps to the ground in a heap
And I pick it all up in a tangle,
Then my pillow resigns and politely declines
To recline at the usual angle.

I know I could just give up and get up. Churchill and Napoleon rarely slept more than four hours and it didn't do them much harm. But I wonder whether they looked like me at the breakfast table —so sluggish I can't get cereal into my mouth without hitting my cheek.

As any insomniac knows, the key to fighting insomnia is to stay in bed, STOP THINKING and go back to sleep. But how? I've tried "sleep tapes" with hypnotic voices ordering me to *relax, relaax, relaaaaaaax.*

I've listened to New Age "soundscapes" of waves, waterfalls and animals going: *Chicicicicica-oooooo. Chicachicacacaca-ooooo ooooo oooooo.*

Many insomniacs I know have their own tricks, which they are eager to share. Some sing tedious songs like "100 Bottles of Beer on the Wall" until they bore themselves to sleep; others repeat mantras like "I am what I am what I am what I am."

One person I know falls asleep by imagining he is falling downward, forever, in a variety of ways. He falls out of planes, buildings, cable cars and double-decker buses; down cliffs, elevators, wells and mine shafts.

I tried it and it kept me up all night.

In the early '70s, I lived in a student co-op with ten people, including a European ambassador's daughter and a male psychiatric intern who wore a skirt. The only thing we all had in common was insomnia.

Every night at 4:30 a.m. we would gather in the kitchen for an informal "Insomnia Clinic." We read aloud numbing poems like T.S. Eliot's "The Wasteland" and brewed a variety of sleep potions: warm milk and honey, hot chocolate and camomile tea, boiled hawthorne berries mixed with valerian root and what looked like the wing of a bat.

None of it helped anyone fall asleep, but it was a lot more fun than lying in bed counting backwards from 10,000.

My only really dependable sleep solution is to read myself back to sleep. I have a bedside library of Insomnia Classics that could knock anyone out— not thrillers or best-sellers, just thick tomes that are the literary equivalent of Nembutol tablets.

Being and Nothingness, by Sartre. *Pelican Life in the Sargasso Archipelago.*

I am always in the market for a good, dull read, so if any of you have a boring book you are no longer using, please send it along to me. With luck, I'll sleep through it.

Car Bazaar

TWO YEARS AGO in Egypt, I spent an afternoon with Mohammed, a carpet salesman, who poured me tea while he gave his sales spiel. He painstakingly explained the weave of each carpet, the number of knots, the dye and design — but there was one piece of information he wouldn't reveal:

The price —which he guarded like the secret of the sphinx.

You can find Mohammed's reincarnation all over North America. Only his name is Al and he sells cars.

To walk into a car dealership is to enter a world without price tags. Buy a toaster, a TV or a tomato, and a price is quickly available — but go to a car dealer and you will never see a pricetag on a car, or anyone willing to reveal it without 45 minutes of negotiations:

Before discussing the cost of any car, Al will insist on showing you the possible "features," which come in two convenient packages:

1: MODEL U-SUCK-R has a mind-boggling list of gadgets: cruise control, cell phone, seat warmer, skyhook and anti-tank rocket missile capacity.

2: MODEL C-A-R is a stripped-down model at half the price. It has no radio, no mats, no window handles, no steering wheel and no doors. And there aren't any models in stock. It is just a theoretical car — and you must build on it like a model car, with Al listing the price of every mudflap.

At some point you will lose your temper and ask Al what it costs for a regular car, "something I can just drive out of here." And Al will pull a number out of the air.

Al: Well Josh, the list price is $17,253.

In the history of Al's car-selling career no one has actually paid the list price. Like Mohammed, Al knows what you will say:

You: OK Al (wink wink), now what's the *real* price?

Al: Oh, you want the *real* price? Well, why don't you come into my office?

Soon you are seated at Al's desk, as he punches a calculator and mumbles numbers to himself. Al has been selling this car every day for a year but he has never actually worked out the price before. He was waiting for you to step in the door.

"Hmmm, let's see, your basic car with an engine and stuff will be hmmmm, (*punch, punch, punch*) — $14,995. Plus transport."

"Transport" is the cost of getting the car to the dealer and assembling it, something you would normally take for granted. But incredibly, this is considered an "extra" cost.

Usually it costs about $895, as you can see in any car ad in the paper, clearly listed beside an asterisk, in fine print, at the bottom of the page:

SPECIAL: ONLY $9995 (* plus transport).

How car companies get away with this is one of the great mysteries of the legal world. It's like a restaurant menu that says:

Fried Chicken —$7.50 (*plus cooking).

Naturally, the cost of transport can be negotiated, along with the number of windshield wipers, headlights and wheels. Periodically during negotiations, Al will go off to "see the manager," and return shaking his head:

"Geez, I'm sorry, he just won't drop more than $150 — but he's willing to throw in a floor mat *and* a coffee holder, today only."

Some people think "the manager" is a fictitious creature, but he is real. If you stand your ground long enough and bargain hard enough, you may actually be invited to meet him and "close the deal." Very few customers last this long.

It's like a video game where, if you score enough points, you confront the Black Prince who guards the final gate. You expect a cross between Darth Vader and Lee Iaccoca, but it's usually just a paunchy, balding guy in a suit, who puts his arm on your shoulder and says: "OK, Josh — I think we can make a deal."

Then the entire process starts over.

Some people claim you can skip the whole exercise by buying from a growing number of car brokers who supposedly tell you the "real price" immediately.

I don't believe it. After my own lengthy foray I've decided that no one actually knows the real price of a car— not even the manufacturers. Sometime, somewhere, someone probably knew it, but he died and forgot to pass it down, and now we are all guessing — like a tribe of cave men which has lost the secret of fire.

That's why no matter how long you bargain, and no matter how "final" the offer, Al's last words as you leave the store to check the price down the street, will always be the same as Mohammed's:

"Come back again, my friend. Maybe I can give you a better price tomorrow."

Air Scare

MY SEATBACK IS IN THE UPRIGHT POSITION, my hand luggage is stowed in front of me and with luck, the cabin temperature will not drop, causing the oxygen mask to fall from the overhead bin and frighten me to death.

As I write, I am 35,000 feet up in the air — about 34,995 feet higher than I am comfortable. I have flown to many places, from the Sahara Desert to the North Pole.

In Bob Hope's words, "I have been almost as many places as my luggage."

Yet no matter how often I fly, I never get used to it. I know that some people are perfectly at ease about flying. They sit by the window, staring out dreamily, oblivious to the fact they are five miles in the air with no visible means of support.

These people are obviously insane — but fortunately, I have a healthy fear of flying.

I think of airplanes as flying Molotov cocktails: fragile vessels filled with explosive fuel, 200 potential terrorists—and me. I hate takeoff, I hate landing and I hate what comes in between, especially if it includes turbulence. My imagination runs wild.

I think about doors that explode and seams that crack, about birds in the propeller, and airlines that go bankrupt and sell off their engines for spare parts, before they land.

And I listen. I listen to the drone of the engine, the creak of the wing flaps and the clunk of the landing gear — alert for sounds the captain may have missed.

"What's that hissing? *Ohmigod*! —There's a hole in the plane!!"

"No — wait — maybe it's just a toilet flushing. Yeah, that's it! We're OK!...But what's that buzzing?"

I also listen to the crew members' voices during flight announcements, trying to detect any secret anxieties.

Do they sound calm? Or edgy? — as if they have been taken hostage?

I know they are trained to hide their feelings. If an engine fell off and the plane dropped like a stone, they would announce:

"The captain has lowered the landing gear. We have now begun our final descent."

My sole comfort is knowing that half the passengers on board are also nervous. Like me, they are all sitting in the aisle seats. Calm travellers sit by the window, staring at the "view" and cooing:

"Oooohh, look at the mountaintops! Aren't they beautiful?"

(No. They prevent making an emergency landing.)

Like other aisle passengers, I never glance at the window. I spend the whole flight staring at the floor and ordering drinks, trying to convince myself I am not really in a plane. I am in a long thin bar that trembles every few minutes when a subway goes by.

If I look out the window, I might see something that breaks the mood: Isn't that an airplane wing? What's it doing outside the bar?

Good afternoon, ladies and gentlemen —

Ah, the captain. He sounds quiet and well-adjusted, not one of those yakky types who frighten you with statistics:

"Our flying time will be 6 hours and 3 minutes at a height of 37,215 feet. Our barometric pressure is 88, with a strong headwind of 75 knots.

"Our wingspan is 38 metres, with engine torque of 450 over 17. My hat size is 7½ and my waist is 34."

If I wanted to know the details of flying, I would be a pilot, not a passenger. And what does he mean by "strong" headwinds, anyway?

Are they *too* strong?

Even worse are honest pilots: "Sorry we took off late, folks. There was a little trouble with the left engine — but we got her patched up and I don't foresee any more difficulty once the glue dries."

I was in a plane at Boston airport two years ago, waiting for takeoff, when the captain walked out of the cockpit carrying a hammer. As I watched in horror, he climbed down the steps, clambered onto the wing and began pounding furiously.

I grabbed my hand luggage and was halfway out the door when I met the captain coming back in.

"Sorry, just a little ice on the wings," he said. "I couldn't get it off so I've called in the ground crew."

He was a nice fellow and persuaded me to sit down again, but the amazing thing was how calm the other passengers were. They wouldn't have blinked if the captain had dragged the wing into the plane and tried to take off without it.

Fortunately for today's flight, they have me on board to look out for things. In fact, writing this story has been distracting me from my duties.

I have doors to check, windows to examine and seams to listen to — before the plane lands. Then I'm off to inspect other flights.

But for now, I think I'd better order another drink. A very long subway seems to be going by.

Electronic Love

HE IS A TYPE X, an electronics engineer who spends his day around "virtual audio consoles" and 100-foot coaxial cable he calls "spaghetti."

She is a Type Y, a bright, creative woman, but technologically-challenged like most of us. Complete opposites, they were naturally attracted.

After several years of going out, they recently bought a house and moved in together, and she found herself trapped in an "Electronic House of Horrors."

Within days of moving in, he had wired up the house like a TV broadcasting studio. She was surrounded by state-of-the-art equipment she could not start to comprehend.

"I'd always programmed my own VCR," she says, "but now I couldn't even play a tape, or turn on the TV. Everything was connected to five speakers, six components and seven remote controls — and I never knew which was connected to what."

Sometimes, when she was home alone, the TV would suddenly go on by itself. When she clicked it off, only the picture would go out; the sound stayed on, at maximum volume, for hours.

Her biggest fear was the alarm system which has to be "armed" whenever leaving the house. The first week she forgot to arm it and the police were there in minutes, along with three close friends automatically called by his security company.

When she arrives home she must "disarm" the system. She has exactly 30 seconds to run up the stairs and punch in her code before security police are alerted.

"I come home clutching four shopping bags and start sweating as soon as I turn the key, because an electronic voice is shouting: *"Alarm System 3 has been activated! Alarm System 3 has been activated!"*

"I drop my shopping bags and run upstairs like a crazy person — but sometimes I'm so nervous I forget my code, and have to rummage through five drawers to find it before the police come. I'm scared I'll have a heart attack."

Her mate is a gentle man. He patiently explained how each system worked, what every cable and jack did, but she didn't understand. He bought her easy-to-follow operating manuals for everything. She fell asleep reading them.

Their electronic relationship was heading for a crisis when he left on a business trip for Chicago. She drove him to Dorval Airport in his car, and before boarding, he reminded her about his car's new alarm system. Did she remember how to use it?

Yes, she said. Before starting the engine, she had to "disarm" the system by waving her hand over a secret spot near the hand brake. "Don't worry," she said, pointing at the spot. "I'm not a complete idiot."

At 10 a.m. he was in the air and she was back in the car, where she waved her hand over the brake and turned the key. Nothing happened. She waved at the brake again and again, then desperately started waving at other things: the steering wheel, the glove compartment, the radio and ashtray.

Twenty minutes later, she marched furiously to a phone booth and called a garage. Soon a towtruck had arrived to haul her car away — but it didn't get far.

The airport parking lot guard wanted to see her car registration, but naturally it was only in *his* name, and he couldn't be reached till late that night. Her driver's license didn't even have the same address. She had moved in only a couple of months earlier and, like many Type Ys, she hadn't gotten around to updating her ID.

A half-hour later she was sitting in an RCMP car, accused of auto theft.

"At first they thought I was a professional car thief — but eventually they decided I'd just had a fight with my boyfriend and was stealing his car as revenge."

At 4 p.m. they released her, without the car. She took a $25 cab home and scoured the house till she found an electricity bill with both their names. Then she taxied back to the aiport and showed it to the RCMP. They released the car.

But by now the garage mechanic had concluded he couldn't start the car either. At 7 p.m., another truck towed the car downtown to her dealer, where she left it in a white rage. She had lost a whole day and $165 in taxis and tows.

At home, she wanted to listen to some music but he wasn't there to help her, so "I just lay in bed in silence, fuming."

Next morning she was back at the dealer, where a mechanic told her the car was fine.

"Great," she said. "What was wrong?"

The mechanic looked embarassed. He didn't like to ask, he said — but was she absolutely sure she knew how to work the alarm?

"Of course," she declared. "You wave your hand over the handbrake then turn the key!"

"Uhhh . . . not exactly," said the man. "I'm afraid you have to turn the key, *then* wave your hand over the handbrake."

"What's the difference?" she asked.

The mechanic sighed.

Since the "crisis" she has started to take charge of her electronic life. She has changed the house alarm code to a number based on her birthday. She has lengthened the police alarm from 30 seconds to 90 seconds, despite protests from the security company. She has slowly learned to use his fax and his phone and is wading her way through a thick manual for his VCR.

"I think I'm getting the hang of it," she says. "If things go well, next week I'm planning to take the big step.

"I'm going to try to master the stereo."

None of the Above

I STILL REMEMBER the fateful exam in grade eight when my history teacher, Mr. Baumgarten, handed out HB pencils and little white cards filled with boxes.

I was confused. Where was the usual essay question?

It was my introduction to "multiple-choice" questions, a terrifying new skill that required precise answers from my fuzzy brain. Answers like:

Why did Napoleon cross the Italians Alps?
1)He wanted to attack Austria
2)He wanted to attack New York
3)He liked skiing and spaghetti

But where, I wondered, was answer 4?

"He was an insecure, short guy who craved power and attention."

At the time, I thought multiple-choice questions were a passing fad. Little did I know I had seen the future and my choices were limited.

Today, the world has gone multiple-choice mad. Exams, questionnaires, polls and government forms are a blur of boxes demanding to know if I am Male, Female or Other?

Married, single or living in sin?

Decisions await me everywhere. My automatic bank machine grills me with questions like:

Do you want to
1)deposit,
2)withdraw,
3)rob the bank?

My personal computer asks me so many questions my memory crashes, and if it doesn't like an answer, it flashes BAD COMMAND as if I was being house-trained.

There is also the spreading "interactive" phone system, which is turning button-pushing into a replacement for conversation. Phone any Quebec government office and a brain-dead voice will offer the following handy selection:

Bonjour!!

-Pour service en Français, appuyez sur le 1.

-For service in English, please phone Ontario.

Stay on the line and you must answer a long series of skill-testing questions, in search of the question you called to ask, but I still have the same problem I did in grade eight:

No matter how many choices I'm offered, I can never find quite the one I want. When I call my car dealer I don't know if I want

1) the repair department,

or,

2) the new parts department.

I want:

3) the department that tells me which department I need.

I rarely know what I want until I've thoroughly discussed what's available.

I know some of you techno-types think the problem isn't multiple-choices — it's me. Like other machine-incompatible people I lag behind the times. I'm too indecisive. Too fuzzy. Too human.

I am an old-fashioned, analogue person, who sees an infinite number of answers to every question. The world needs digital people — a new species that can reduce any question in life to five possible answers. Soon we will be seeing:

INTER-WAITRESS:

There'll be no place for indecisive orders like: "Uhhh, I'll have one egg, over easy, on toast, *very* lightly buttered, with potatoes on the side but NOT touching my eggs."

With Inter-Waitress your restaurant experience will sound like this:

Inter-Waitress: You have selected — eggs. Do you want your eggs
1) scrambled,
2) poached,
3) fried?

Customer: Uh, over easy with hard yolks.
Inter-Waitress: BAD COMMAND. Please place your order again.

INTER-ANALYST:
Tell me, Mr. Smith. Do you avoid intimacy in relationships through:
1)work,
2)casual sex,
3)watching TV,
4)interactive telephone relationships?

INTER-DOCTOR:
Thank you for dialing Inter-doctor's Cardiac Clinic. If you are experiencing chest pains, listen carefully.
For dull, periodic pain, press 1.
For throbbing pain and nausea, press 2.
For severe, stabbing pains and dizziness, press 3.
(Beep).
You have NOT selected a button. Please Press 1, 2 or 3 now.
Please select now.
(Beep).
Sorry, this call is terminated.

That's why I'm doing my best to become a multiple-choice personality before it's too late. In fact, I'm experimenting with a new, interactive answering machine message of my own:

Hi. Thanks for calling Inter-Josh.
To invite me to parties and social engagements, press 1.
To discuss work, press 2.
To discuss bills, taxes or complaints about things I have written, press 3.
An operator will be with you as soon as Napoleon arrives in New York.

No English (9 a.m.- 5 p.m.)

April 3, 1993
Conseil de la Langue Française
Department of Silly Signs

Thanks for launching the latest phase of Operation Language Storm, the policy that helps Quebecers forget unemployment and bankruptcy and focus on the big problems of life — signs.

Earlier operations, like Bill 101 and Bill 178, distracted us for years, but those battles were waning until you boldly stepped in to propose a sillier sign law. You want to permit English signs in small shops, as long as they're only half the size of French signs. And you want to prohibit them in big shops.

Bravo! This should keep English storekeepers in court for years, battling over the size of their businesses, while French nationalists yell that every English business is big business.

It should keep teams of language inspectors busy measuring signs like "JUMBO DELI" to make sure the letters are only half the size of the ones in the French version —"DELI JUMBO."

Your proposal is admirably silly — but still — is it silly enough to sustain the never-ending debate to which Quebecers are accustomed? Let me offer some sign-law suggestions of my own, guaranteed to infuriate everyone for years:

BILL OO7: This plan would permit English signs, but give prominence to French by making the letters bigger, brighter, bolder, more beautiful.

For instance, we could allow French words in color but English ones only in black on white. Or better still, in black on black.

We could also handicap English so it's hard to read, by requiring words to be written upside down —or backwards! Signs like S'NEB, or S'ZTRAWHS and S'YARRUM could be understood by Anglos without disturbing French ultra-nationalists.

As could NRAB-B-RAB, PELUJ EGNARO and ENITUOP FO NEEUQ EHT.

BILL 5:00-7:00 (Happy hour): Many anglos have argued for linguistic zones, allowing bilingual signs in the west end of Montreal and French ones in the east. But this is residential discrimination.

Why not just allow everyone to put up English signs at certain times of the week, designated as "English hours"? Signs would be posted on every street, stating when English was and wasn't permitted. For instance:

PAS D'ANGLAIS
Lundi - Vendredi
9 a.m. - 5 p.m.

English signs left out during those hours would be ticketed by English Onions, and towed away to the pound by a company called "Affichage Québécois."

BILL 100% Français: Every word would be in French — period. Sure, it's harsh but at least all signs would be treated equally unfairly. No more of those half-English signs that mar the city's French Look — like Le Roi du Hot Dog, Le Shed and Le Swimming. No more U.S. companies like Dunkin' Donuts and Burger King selling "le whopper," and "l'oeuf McMuffin."

No more Monsieur Nice Guy.

Car dealers would no longer be able to put up big English signs advertising "Oldsmobile." Instead, they'd sell a "Viellemobile," as well as an "Oiseau de Feu" and a "Royce Roulant."

Quebecers would shop at "Pneu Canadien" and drink soft drinks like "7- En-Haut." And I would write this column for *Le Montreal Petrolette,* not *The Gazette,* and sign it with a good French version of my name:

"Blague Liberée" — Joke Freed.

BILL 100% English: In the 1960s Montreal signs were mainly in English and look what they produced: Gilles Vigneault, Pauline Julien and an angry young generation of francophones who practically refused to speak English.

Since the late 1970s, we've had all-French sign laws and what's been the result?: Céline Dion, Mitsou and a host of other Quebecers who sing in English. That's what happens when you have too much security.

All-English signs would be a constant reminder that French-Quebecers are a tiny island of French in a sea of English. The linguistic insecurity would provoke decades of political rallies and a never-ending wave of

French songs, plays and movies.

If a clever nationalist government suppressed every sign of French, the plan could quickly result in independence — a sovereign French nation, eternally kept on its guard by the English sign at the border:

"Welcome to Quebec."

N.B. Any of the above laws should cause enough debate to distract us for years. But don't expect anglo storeowners to change their signs quickly, no matter what the law.

It took almost ten years for them to obey Bill 101 and not because they're anti-French. Most just couldn't be bothered with the time and expense — and they won't this time either.

Frankly, I don't think most anglo shopkeepers even care whether they have English signs anymore. They'd just like to know they could if they wanted to.

Yours truly,

Blague Liberée

North to Nowhere

OUR MUNICIPAL GOVERNMENT is posting brightly-colored City maps all over downtown. They may help tourists, but they're just one more thing to confuse me next time I'm lost.

I am cartographically-challenged. Directionally-disabled. Lost in space. Every time I step out of an elevator, I turn the wrong way. Every time I leave a building I forget how I got there. Every direction looks the same to me — and geez — where did I park the car?

Some people are born with an inner compass, but I got a roulette wheel instead — and it always seems to be spinning. Abandon me in the middle of a department store and I may never find my way out.

"Attention shoppers! Would the mother of a tall male please pick him up at the information desk. He is bald and bearded, and answers to the name Josh."

I've always envied people with a sense of direction. Drop them into a new city, and within an hour they know exactly where everything is:

"Hmmm, so the river runs north-south and the streets work on a north-west by southeast grid, centred around the old city. Great, let's go to Chinatown. It's that way."

People like this love to look at maps, savoring every squiggle as if they were driving on it.

"Wow! Look at the elevation on this road! It rises westward off the Chakiwaki River then cuts right over Interstate 95!"

They never get lost and are boring to travel with because they know about every lake and mountain before they get to it.

"Look! A moose!" you'll shout.

"I know," they'll reply, with a yawn. "I saw it on the map a half hour ago."

Like all directionally-disabled people, I hate maps, because they make me feel inadequate. When I open them they flap around in the wind. When I fold them, they look like crumpled Kleenex.

When I look at them, I get dizzy, numbed by all the lines, dots and incomprehensible symbols. Normal people look at a map and see the four cardinal points: N-S-E-W. But I look at a map and see four completely different directions:

U-D-R-L: Up, Down, Right and Left.

The Arctic is Up and the U.S. is Down. British Columbia is Out Left and the Atlantic Ocean is Out Right. To stay oriented I have to keep turning the map around so it faces where I'm going — not easy when you're on the Décarie Circle.

Like most cartographically-challenged people, I get nervous in the woods. Every tree looks the same and there are no street names — there aren't even any gas stations to ask directions. I feel safer in cities, where there's someone at every bus stop to give me advice:

"You're looking for the airport? OK, you go left at the third intersection, then hang a right at the railway tracks and bear left at the fourth street after the second flashing light.

"And remember — if you go through a very long tunnel, you've passed it."

(Translation: Drive three blocks then ask someone else for directions.)

This is known as the query-and-quest method of navigation, and it's usually effective. If you keep driving and ask enough people for help, eventually one of them will say:

"The airport? This *is* the airport."

Admittedly, asking directions can cause trouble in some countries, where people feel it is polite to help you even when they don't know how.

"Oh yes, the town of El Dahib is that way," they will say cheerfully and wish you a safe two-day journey, although they have never heard of the place.

There are also countries where people consider it rude to point, so they give directions by waving in a circular motion that can lead you anywhere.

But other places make it easier to get around. Some Toronto suburbs order their streets alphabetically, giving them names like Apple, Blossom, Cherry and Daisy.

Many American cities like Manhattan, in New York, number their streets and avenues, so you just keeping counting till you get to 75th Street and 5th Avenue. Yes, it lacks poetry, and is a bit like living in a numbered cellblock, but at least I can find my hotel.

Then there's Montreal, where the streets are all cockeyed, because they were laid out perpendicular to the river, not on north-south lines. It's the only city in North America where the sun rises in the south and sets in the north, and nothing is where you think it is.

Look at a Quebec map and the famous West End district of Westmount is deep in the East End. Sherbrooke Street, the city's major east-west axis runs north-south, and "Upnorth" is really out west.

Yet Montreal is not the hardest city to get around. That distinction probably goes to Tokyo, where incredibly there are *no* street names. And most addresses are not in any order.

The number on a house tells you *when* it was built, not where it is on the street, so getting around Tokyo is an art form, not a science. Dinner hosts have you picked up by hired car, or provide a calling card complete with a printed map. Even veteran cabbies will stop a dozen times along the way to discuss the destination with neighborhood residents who debate it heatedly, while the meter runs.

The philosophy behind this seems to be based on privacy: Why advertise your home's whereabouts to strangers? If someone doesn't know where you live, he has no business visiting you.

Not surprisingly, when the U.S. army occupied Japan after World War II, they tried to "civilize" Tokyo, by giving orderly names to all the downtown streets — English names like First Street and Avenue A.

Not surprisingly, the Japanese ignored the signs which have slowly rusted away or vanished, leaving the streets nameless again. It seems that most Japanese prefer not to know exactly where they are going.

Which makes me feel right at home.

Unintelligence Briefing

SOME PEOPLE SAY HUMAN BEINGS don't use 90 percent of their brain's potential intelligence — but I've never felt that's a big problem. The real waste is the 90 percent of artificial intelligence we don't use in the electronic world around us.

Take my new computer, which boasts a 20-megabyte, 16-MHz memory — whatever that means. It's a tiny lap-sized machine with all kinds of wondrous features, the product of 500,000 years of human evolution.

Unfortunately there is a weak link in the circuit — me.

Like most computer users, I ignore the sophisticated things my machine can do and use it like a typewriter, bashing away as if it were a 1920 Underwood. Often, while I'm typing, it seems to gets bored and flashes messages like:

"Would you like to build a library-merge file?"

"No," I type, having absolutely no idea what it is talking about. And soon it flashes other messages.

"How about accessing A: MERGE/B/files/doc/With BLT/MAYO/FRIES/LARGE COKE?"

Last week when I entered my office and turned on the computer, I thought I saw the screen flash: "God, not this dolt again."

Who can blame it? It is like a Nobel laureate forced to spend life in a classroom run by a kindergarten student.

"OK, Mr. Einstein, how much is 2 minus 1 times 2?"

The same waste of intelligence applies to the simplest electronic machines that litter our planet, tragically wasting their potential. In the movie *City Slickers*, two fat-cat executives are out on a wilderness horseback trip, discussing the larger questions of modern life:

"The big thing I can never really figure out," says one, "is how you can tape one show on your VCR while you're watching another? Also, how do you set the clock?"

The line sent most of the audience into howls of laughter, which obviously meant no one in the theatre had any idea how to set their VCR clock either.

My electronic household is a graveyard of unused intelligence. My Auto-Dial-Ease-A-Phone makes me uneasy, since I lost the instruction book telling me how to program in new phone numbers and erase old ones.

It keeps calling Pascal's Hardware, which has been out of business for three years.

My car radio comes with a sophisticated gadget that immediately "decodes" if a thief steals it, making it impossible to use unless you know the code. Unfortunatly the radio "de-coded" during a cold spell last winter, and I don't know the code either. I haven't used it since.

My computer printer seems frustrated. It is always asking if I want to use other "fonts," like "Helvetica dark" or "Danish light." I prefer Jarlsberg or a good cheddar.

My fax machine has more buttons than NASA control. It can send documents to the furthest reaches of the planet and shrink them to the size of postage stamps. It is always flashing a message encouraging me to:

"Try my polling function." (I think it works for the federal government).

I have never even glanced at this arsenal of features. All I know is that when the machine makes a loud whining noise, I take my index finger and push the big green button that says "START."

If that doesn't work, I put the documents in the mail.

Sometimes I think my electronic household would be better off with a different kind of owner, someone who appreciates its potential. You know: one of those high-tech types who don't buy machines to use them — only to see whether they can master them.

Ask them whether they can record a show for you on their VCR and they say:

"Hah! I have 400-channel, 105-country automatic programming capacity up until the year 2035. If I move to Borneo for five years, I can leave the machine behind and tape every episode of *Wheel of Fortune* while I'm gone."

An owner like this would spend days testing my computer's most obscure functions.

"Ah! A program to translate documents from Welsh into Romanian and Esperanto — just what I need!"

This owner would program my fax to run a polling agency and my watch to play "O Canada" on July 1. My printer would lead an exotic, challenging life, though it might also be a brief one.

Eventually, this type of person always discovers something their gadget cannot do, and someone else's can. Within days, the gadget is in the electronic junkyard, jilted for a new partner with more attractive features.

So take note, my electronic roommates: there may be an advantage to living with a dullard like me, too unadventurous for new flings. You may never reach your potential, but at least you'll be around to have one.

The Gull War

I. BATTLE ON THE POOP DECK

I RETURNED TO MONTREAL after a short absence to discover some disgusting new neighbors had moved into my building: a flock of pigeons that had nested under my back balcony.

They seem to be homing pigeons, and unfortunately, their home is my home.

They awake at 4:30 a.m. and flap around outside my bedroom window, making loud cooing sounds that penetrate the best earplugs money can buy. They crash against my windows. They perch on my bannisters and poop on my balcony, as if it were a public toilet. They have turned my house into a scene from Hitchcock's *The Birds*. Friends who have been through this problem all give me the same advice:

"Kill them," said a gentle, young law student, forced out of her home last year by pigeons.

"Poison them and eat them," said a vegetarian friend.

I would, if I could get at them. I fantasize about BB guns, poison darts and pet falcons. They have brought out a dark, murderous impulse in me, and I would like to satisfy it.

I was not always prejudiced against the pigeon. A few years ago I wrote a naive ode to this "noble, urban bird."

"Pity the poor pigeon," I wrote at the time. "Home owners chase it, professionals poison it. Yet the pigeon is a true Montrealer who lives in our city because he wants to — not because he's on a leash.

"Unlike the heralded Canada goose, the pigeon doesn't just vacation here in summer. He is a real Canadian, who sticks it out all winter."

What twaddle. In the past two weeks I have learned a lot more about pigeons than I knew back then, and none of it is good. I am locked in a turf war with a flock of 50 birds and I am being outmuscled.

Actually, these pigeons don't even come in a flock. They are more like a street gang — a nasty, aggressive bunch of delinquents — the Hell's Angels of the bird world. They are led by a fat, aggressive white bird I have named Attila, who plops down on my bannister to poop whenever he pleases, then shrieks for the rest of his horde to follow.

Attila is a tough bird, with attitude. I tried to chase him off with a broom, but he didn't back down; he squawked and fluttered until I fled into the house.

Unnerved, I changed tactics. I spent all last Wednesday crouched behind the balcony door, watching. Whenever Attila and his pals landed, I leaped out and hurled a basketball down my balcony, like a bowling ball, trying for a 10-pigeon strike.

"Scram!" I'd shout, shaking my fist as they scattered to a neighbor's roof. "Get it through your bird brains — this is *my* balcony!"

I figured a few episodes like this would teach them to poop elsewhere, but after three days they were more brazen than ever. My friend who'd been forced out of her home by pigeons explained the problem:

"It's hopeless," she said. "You can't train them — because they don't learn. They're too stupid."

This was bad news. Suddenly I could see into the mind of my enemy and there was nothing there. I tried to imagine the scenario from Attila's point of view:

He is perched on my neighbor's roof and spots another pigeon.

- Hi! I'm Attila. Who are you?
- I'm Genghis. Nice to meet you.
- OK, Genghis, see that balcony with the bald guy hiding behind the door? Let's go poop on it!
- Yeah!

They land on the balcony, and five seconds later a huge basketball comes out of nowhere, flattening them for the 500th time. They flee back to the roof, terrified:

Attila: Geez, that was a close one!
Genghis: Yeah, we'd better stay away from that lunatic's balcony.

Ten more seconds go by — a decade in the mind of a pigeon — then the two birds look at each other again.

- Hi! I'm Attila. Who are you?
- I'm Genghis. Nice to meet you.
- OK, Genghis, see that balcony with the bald guy hiding behind the door? Let's go poop on it!

- Yeah!

My enemy suffers from a permanent case of pigeon Alzheimer's, I realized. It was time for more desperate measures. Several days ago, my brother Mike, our family's technical expert, came in with a mask and an arsenal of anti-pigeon equipment.

He searched out and destroyed their empty nest, boarded up the spot where it had been, and installed thin piano wire along every bannister, making it impossible to perch.

Homeless, the birds went wild, shrieking, flapping and fleeing to the neighbor's roof. They peered wistfully down at my balcony, making glum sounds and looking at me like I was a home-wrecker.

I guess I am. *Heh, heh.*

Yesterday morning, I came out on my balcony and there wasn't a bird to be seen on the bannister. They were building a new nest, *on* my balcony. *Sigh.*

As I write, my brother is out sealing off the entire 12-foot-high balcony in more piano wire. Soon, he will be installing other anti-pigeon paraphernalia: pinwheels, fake owls and snakes, a floor spray that will sting the pigeons' feet. Maybe even broken glass, razor wire and land mines. He assures me the pigeons will not be able to use my back balcony any more, though unfortunately neither will I.

We are in a standoff.

My wired-up balcony looks like a prison camp and every window in my house is sealed shut. As I write, the pigeons are flying around the back courtyard, shrieking and beating on the piano wire. They can't get in, and I can't go out. Frankly, I'm not really sure who has won. I suspect Attila and Genghis are talking:

Genghis: Where's the bald guy? He hasn't been around today.
Attila: Don't worry about him. We finally got him caged.

CHAPTER TWO

Health Scare

Rest in Grease

R.I.P.
POPCORN: (3000 B.C. - 1994)
May You Rest In Grease.

LOS ANGELES — For years, Serge Losique, boss of the Montreal World Film Festival, banned popcorn from his theatres — probably the only moviehouses in the world with this policy.

It turns out Losique was saving movie buffs from early death. He foresaw the future, when popcorn would prove to be the *Terminator* of the junk-food world, the *Killer Kernel of Cinema Snacks*.

According to a Washington research group: Popcorn Is Hazardous To Your Health. They found that a medium-sized "buttered" popcorn has more fat than a bacon-and-eggs breakfast, *plus* a Big-Mac-with-fries lunch and a large steak dinner.

It's probably healthier to eat the carton and throw the popcorn away.

Movie theatre spin doctors are trying to contain the study's damage, like squirming tobacco executives arguing that cigarettes are good for losing weight. But they're fighting a losing battle. Our society is obsessed by fear of soft stomachs and hard arteries, and popcorn suddenly has the smell of bypass surgery.

To be fair, it's not really popcorn that's unhealthy — it's the coconut cooking oil used to make it. But details be damned. Now that Fear of Popcorn has started, there'll be no popping it. Let us mourn popcorn's passing — the latest in a long series of junk-food victims to be assassinated by studies.

Like burgers, bacon, butter, fries, hot dogs, chips, chocolate, eggs, salt, sugar, steak, sausage, sour cream and anything else with taste, popcorn will soon be passé.

Walk into a deli for a smoked meat these days and friends look at you like you were entering a brothel. Ask for a regular Coke and people stare as if you asked for leaded gasoline.

A friend was recently told his children can no longer bring junk-food to school for lunch, not even a Coffee Crisp. Or a bag of Miss Vickie's chips. Or popcorn.

The motto of our times is "Eat, Drink and Be Wary."

As the era of junk-food comes to an end, I for one, mourn:

I've been a junk-food addict since I was old enough to scarf sausage, a fast-food connoisseur in search of the best junk that food can provide.

I have sampled every new development, from whole-wheat pizza and chili nachos to the short-lived McRib— the Edsel of the fast-food world. I have dined on the Wilensky's Special, the Dilallo Buckburger, the indescribable Mr. Pogo.

I was the first Montrealer, west of St. Laurent Blvd., to try poutine, a Quebec concoction made of french fries smothered in cheese curds and barbecue sauce. I have spent hours debating the merits of the thin french fry vs. the thick one, and whether it should be eaten with ketchup, mayonnaise or paprika and vinegar.

I have driven all the way to Burlington, Vermont just to eat the hash browns at Henry's Diner. I could write a paean to pizza, a love letter to the latke, a sonnet to the steamed hot dog:

> *A cup of Coke, a soggy bun and thee*
> *O steamie.*

The first inkling I had that junk-food was in jeopardy came about a decade ago, when Wendy's became the first fast-food joint to introduce a salad bar. Broccoli and celery spears in a burger joint? — it was like holding a baptism in a bar.

Soon, "fresh garden salads" had spread insidiously from Burger King to Harvey's, along with "low-cal" chicken burgers, 2-per cent milkshakes and "fat-free" yogurt. Then came the McLean, a burger made with "seaweed extract" that had even less taste than McDonald's regular burger.

As fear of food spread in the 1980s, about the only guilt-free junk left at the snack counter was popcorn — thought to be low in calories. Sure, we knew that weird yellow "topping" couldn't be *good* for us — but who knew it was the agent orange of the cinema world?

I can see the future and I don't want to be there.

Theatre chains will fight back with new "diet popcorns," cooked in yogurt and fresh seawater — and enhanced with fat-fighting vitamins. But popcorn paranoia will continue to spread, including the fear of side aroma from people eating the real thing.

Health zealots will demand "No Popcorn" sections in every theatre. Soon, there will be "No Popcorn" theatres, then no popcorn, period. Addicts will be pressured to switch to corn chips, the methadone of the popcorn world, and popcorn will become a controlled substance, with mandatory warnings on every carton:

DANGER: Eat With Caution.
Popcorn Can Reduce Life Expectancy.

The same fate awaits other junk foods. There will be T-shirts saying "Burger-free Body," while police give junkalyzer tests to catch motorists who are hyped-up on sugar or beef. Car insurance forms will ask:

"Have you consumed any drugs, tranquilizers or junk-food in the last year?"

By the year 2000, chemists will have phased out junk-food entirely. Fast-food diners of the future will go to a Sprout King restaurant and order like this:

"Gimme two steambeans all dressed, an algaeburger on 9-grain and a fresh fry-free. And which way is the No Ketchup section, please?"

Eventually someone may re-market "junk-food," but only in milder form — say, popcorn-flavored vitamin pills that you gulp down at movies, along with Vitamin B(utter) and Vitamin C(oke).

Ten years from now, during exciting moments of a film, you will no longer hear the rustle of 300 popcorn bags — only the sound of 300 vitamin bottles opening, followed by a whispered:

"Pass the Perrier pills, please."

Junk Mail Memory

I HAVE ALWAYS HAD AN EXCELLENT MEMORY for things I would love to forget.

I remember my address when I was five years old: 8133 de l'Épée, apt. 3. I remember the date of the Battle of Hastings: 1066 —though I can never recall just what happened there.

I can rattle off the Lord's Prayer by heart from my public school days, although I suspect I may have had some of the words wrong: (Our-father-who-art-in-heaven-halibut-be-thine-name).

Fragments of useless information swirl through my brain like space debris, most of them so trivial I can't even use them for *Trivial Pursuit*. They take up so much of my memory, there's no room left for things that are useful.

I can't remember what day to take out the garbage. I never remember what side of my street to park on. It takes me 15 minutes to find my car after a movie and fifteen more to remember where I put the keys. And while I recently managed to write out a list of the birthdays I always forget, I can't remember where I put the list.

In a world of junk food, junk mail and junk bonds, I have a junk memory.

I am not alone. The planet is full of people who selectively forget important facts and only retain useless ones. Some of them never forget a joke, but always forget they've told it to you.

Others never forget your name, although they have no idea who you are. (They usually become politicians).

I've known middle-aged women who recall exactly what you wore to their 16th birthday party: "It was that ocean-green tweed jacket and those *dreadful* penny loafers."

"But I don't recall your name."

There are men who remember sports trivia like scientists remember formulas. They can tell you how many shots on net Jean Beliveau had in the first period of the second game of the 1957 Bruin series; how many steps Roger Bannister took to crack the four-minute mile.

But they can't remember the date of their wedding anniversary or the age of their only child.

Fortunately, I don't waste valuable mental space on foolish things like sports statistics. Instead, I specialize in telephone numbers, a field in which I am practically an idiot savant.

Tell me a phone number and it sticks in my mind like flypaper, years after the number has been disconnected. RE 7-2833 was my number in 1957, until we moved to RE 1-3126 a year later.

VI 4-0111 was the number to call for the correct time in 1968, while CR 7-2115 was my corner pizza joint. CR 7-2196 was Sam Kershinsky's telephone number in public school, although I don't have a clue who Sam was. I never remember a face but I rarely forget a phone number.

"Hey! — 646-7653 — How are you? I haven't seen you in years."

I would love to trade in some old phone numbers for something useful, but unlike my computer, my memory has no delete button and there's no room left on my disc.

Why can't I be like those people who only remember important facts. Argue with them and they say: "Well, you're obviously totally wrong. According to the Potter-Shmellington task force, the GNP of Burundi has fallen by 23 percent in the last three months alone, compared to that of Burkina Faso."

They can always pick a handy quote out of the air from Lord Byron or someone who somehow said exactly what they've been saying all along.

"As Pliny the Elder said in 56 A.D.: "Free trade or no trade."

The only quotes I remember are rhyming couplets, like the theme song of the Walt Disney show that went:

> Texas John Slaughter made'em do what they ought'er,
> And if they didn't they'd die.

And while I can't remember much Shakespeare or Tennyson I'll never forget that "you'll wonder where the yellow went when you brush your teeth with Pepsodent."

As a youngster, my greatest feat of learning was to memorize a vast idiotic poem, almost 80 verses long, that still stalks the corridors of my memory. It has something to do with an old sailor who was shipwrecked, and eventually had to eat every member of his crew. The chorus is:

> Oh, I am the cook and the captain bold,
> And the mate of the Nancy Brig.
> And the bosun tight and the midshipmite
> and the crew of the captain's gig.

45

I still know about 45 stanzas of this silly epic, but I can't remember how it ends. I would look it up, but I can't remember the title, the author or where I learned it.

So if anyone out there specializes in remembering the ending of poems but always forgets the chorus, please give me a call. Maybe we can trade memories.

Hair Today ...

I WAS OUT WITH SOME FRIENDS recently when I mentioned that I had lots of work to "get out of my hair." There was an embarrassed silence, before everyone at the table started giggling.

"Well," said one friend, staring at my shiny pate. "I guess that won't take you very long."

I am hair-impaired, or follicly-challenged as they'd put it today. The top of my head is so smooth you could roll cigarettes on it, my forehead so bare it causes glare.

When meeting strangers in crowded places, I always tell them to look for "the big bald guy." And they always find me.

I know this is a taboo subject for many men, but not me. Sure, hair keeps out snow in winter and is fun to curl round your fingers — but bald isn't all that bad either.

It saves on haircuts, it doesn't get soaked in the rain, and my hair never turns grey, because it usually falls out first.

And I'm in good company. From Socrates and Hippocrates through Caesar and Shakespeare, the history of the hairless is nothing to cover up — though many have tried. Napoleon combed his hair forwards. Churchill combed it sideways. De Gaulle usually wore a hat.

Mozart and Washington always wore wigs.

Theories of what causes baldness have varied too. Socrates thought it was caused by too much sex and Aristotle by not enough. Other people have blamed it on small hats, tight neckties and even too much laughter which "tightens the skin and cuts off blood to the scalp."

Don't laugh.

The bald truth is that two out of three men eventually lose their hair and very few of them like it. I started going bald in my early twenties and it took some time to get used to. Like most men, I tried brushing the sides over the top for a while — what Quebecers refer to as "Lévesquing" your hair, after René Lévesque.

For years my barber chased my part steadily down my head looking for something to plaster on top. Finally, during one visit, he asked:

"Have you ever considered combing your hair back?"

"*Back?*" I said. "But what would go on top?"

It was a pivotal moment in my life. Fifteen minutes later I was officially bald and I haven't retreated since. For a while however, I looked
into miracle cures, of which there are many.

The first recorded medical prescription in history dates back to 4000
B.C., a cure for baldness, written in hieroglyphics, that contains "asses
hooves, dates and bear paws ground together in an earthen jug."

People have been churning out recipes ever since. A British survey
shows most inventors spend their time looking for ways for men to
grow hair. (The rest spend their time looking for schemes for women
to remove hair — the female equivalent to men's obsession with keeping it).

None of these methods do men much good. Nothing convinced me
of this more than a CBC documentary I did on baldness some years ago.

The research took me across North America on a quest for hair. Along
the way, I tested miracle products of every description — from Hair in
a Hurry to Bare Today, Hair Tomorrow. I visited Pennsylvania, where a
70-year-old woman ran a virtual Lourdes for thousands of hairless pil-
grims who sought her help.

I visited a hair replacement salon where I was outfitted with a $1500
hairpiece. It made me look like a mop with legs. I watched a hair
transplant, a grim procedure where holes are drilled in the person's
scalp, then filled in with tufts of flesh from elsewhere on their body. I'd
rather have a root canal.

I saw people zapped with electricity and pelted with cathode rays. I
was covered in a potion containing 22 secret ingredients brewed in a
vat of Seagram's whisky. I tried bear grease, bee's honey and a hormone
pill that grows some hair on some heads some of the time.

None of these methods grew a hair on me. The truth is that baldness
is caused by an excess of male hormones and the only sure-fire remedy
is castration.

Uh, no thanks.

At the end of my odyssey I knew that hair was not for me. The happi-
est people I'd met along the way were members of The Bald-Headed
Men of America, a group of eggheads, based in Morehead, Carolina.
Its 10,000 members are convinced that "skin is in" — that bald heads
are in the "forefront of fashion." They hold an annual beauty pageant
where they select the roundest head, the cuddliest head and the "perfect 10."

The man who won the pageant the year I was there was John T. Capp

III, whose rippling pate is to baldness what Schwarzenegger's pectorals are to muscles. Capp taught me a poem I still recall when bushy-headed people give me a hard time:

> *The lord is just*
> *The lord is fair*
> *He gave some men brains*
> *And the others hair.*

Take My Polls

PLEASE RESPOND.

I am reading this story because:

a) I read it every week.
b) I saw the title and thought it was about something serious for a change.
c) I have already stopped reading it.
d) I'll give it one more paragraph, but it better improve.

Census Day has come and gone — an X-ray of our national soul — but 81.3% of Canadians barely noticed. They were too busy paying attention to all the other polls X-raying their national soul. Every day a new survey appears, measuring how we drink and think, date, mate and hate.

There are polls about:

Geography: 42% of Canadian students think Hudson Bay is a department store. 37% of American tourists think Canada is a U.S. national park.

Culture: 80% of English Canadians think French actress Marina Orsini is an Italian yacht club. 80% of francophones think John A. MacDonald is a low-tar cigarette.

Leisure: 68% of Canadians prefer snow-shovelling to sex. 58% of men are against making condoms available in high school, but in favor of wearing them on their heads at New Year's Eve parties.

There are newspaper polls which take weekly readership surveys on important personal questions like:

"My husband is a loud-mouthed slob who hogs the sheets and snores like an outboard motor, but he's useful to have around for reaching objects high on shelves.

"Agree or disagree?"

Here in Quebec, we are the most polled people in the world, according to recent polls. We have twice as many polls per capita as other people and the questions they ask us get more complicated all the time.

In the past, pollsters simply wanted to know if we were for or against Quebec independence. Now they are delving deeper. Recently, a five-part syndicated newspaper poll examined "The Brain of the Quebecer," probing into the darkest crevices of our political psyche.

When you dream, are you still a federalist, or do you harbour secret separatist fantasies? Are you a Committed Undecided, or an Indecisive Undecided?

Are you more apt to have sexual fantasies about Preston Manning or about Jacques Parizeau? Both together?

The polls were accompanied by a mind-numbing array of charts, pies, and five-color graphics that overwhelmed the eye and brain. In the end we knew so much that we knew nothing.

All polls are accompanied by asterisk warnings saying things like:

"This poll is valid within 19/20 times and reflects the opinions you would give an absolute stranger who telephoned you on Mar. 13, 1994, interrupting you during a fight over who burned the TV dinner."

And yet, like most people, I avidly read every poll to make sure that I'm normal. Do I do as many pushups as other Canadians of my age, sex, and shoe size? Do I floss my teeth as regularly, change my sheets as often, sneeze, snooze and booze as much?

Do I fit in?

The other day a U.S. poll on dietary habits revealed that I eat less fruit than 63.6% of North Americans — so I ran out to stock up on apples. The next day a poll of U.S. dieticians showed that apples have far less nutritional value than previously thought.

Please respond:

    a) Yes, I am still reading this story — but Lord knows why.
    b) No, I'm just browsing. Where are the baseball scores?
    c) This really is my last paragraph. Well, maybe I'll try one more.

Most families I know have appointed a designated poll person whose job is to fill out all questionnaires. Generally the woman is stuck with this task, though the husband stands helpfully by, saying:

"OK Mary, give them my opinion. Tell them what I think."

Yet despite the plague of polls, somehow, I have never been polled. Over the years all manner of strangers have showed up on my doorstep:

chocolate-bar hustlers, Jehovah's Witnesses, bailiffs, postmen, knife sharpeners, real-estate agents, police officers, bag ladies, Denver Booters and men who want to cut off my phone line.

But never a pollster.

Why not? Why don't the Neilsen Ratings people ever ask me what TV programs I watch? Why don't the United Agricultural Producers ask me to name my favorite vegetable? What's wrong with my opinion?

Even in the Census, the twice-in-a-decade opportunity for every last Canadian to express their opinion, I got the short form: a few easy questions about my name, age and sex, then the kiss-off. Why didn't I get to answer all the interesting questions about my mortage payments, my Hydro bills and my "ethnicity."

Am I too ordinary? — the Type-O positive of the polling world — too dreary to study? Is *my brain* less interesting than that of other Quebecers?

Or am I too weird to survey, so marginal that pollsters fear I might skew their results? Am I too typical, or too atypical?

If any of you out there are pollsters, I want you to know I am available to be surveyed. Ask me anything and I promise I'll give any answer you want.

Please respond:

a) Believe it or not, I'm still here.
b) Don't be flattered. I just scanned to the end.
c) This is definitely my last paragraph — and this time I'm not bluffing.

Remain Calm!!!

IT WAS I A.M. and I was just settling into a comfortable Ottawa hotel room when a screaming noise sent me leaping from my chair. A bell clanged madly and a booming voice announced:

"May I have your attention, please! May I have your attention!" Of course it could. The voice was *inside* my bedroom.

"The alarm you are hearing indicates a problem on the 14th floor," shouted the voice. "Follow the instructions on the back of your guest-room door. The alarm you are hearing indicates a problem on the 14th floor . . ."

I was on the 10th floor, but I rushed to the door to read the instructions. But which ones? The double-occupancy fee structure? The Save Electricity guidelines? Or the long list of yellowed paper with fine print I had to squint to read:

"IN CASE OF FIRE. SECT. 3, STATUTE 21 OF THE ONTARIO INNKEEPERS ACT. No innkeeper shall be liable to make good for any property ... not being a horse or other live animal, etc... ."

I turned to yet another set of instructions:

"In case of fire, leave room ... and REMAIN CALM."

Calm? The voice in my room was practically hysterical.

Since I was already dressed, I didn't dawdle. I scanned the room for "valuables" and grabbed what seemed to matter: my wallet, my notepad and a detective novel, in case it was a long night.

Then I rushed down 10 flights of stairs because the elevator wasn't working.

I emerged into the lobby, puffing, to find a scene out of a Fellini film. About 30 people were gathered on the posh hotel sofas, wearing a bizarre collection of attire.

There was a man in a natty beige raincoat and nothing else. An elderly couple in matching striped pyjamas had bare feet. Several people wore bathrobes and dress shoes — but no socks.

"I almost had a heart attack when that bell went," said a woman in a skimpy negligee carrying a bulging purse. "I jumped out of bed, grabbed what I could and ran for my life!"

Her friend in the next room had been more composed: "The second I woke up, I knew exactly what to do. I always memorize the emergency exits as soon as I step into a hotel or a plane.

"I put everything important into my purse and took my agenda ... but I didn't even glance at my clothing. I knew the insurance would cover that!"

One woman grabbed her glasses but overlooked her pearl necklace — "my most valuable possession." Another lugged down two suitcases along with two kids.

Men had different priorities. Many had sports jackets flung over their pyjamas like a seal of respectability. Others had pyjama bottoms poking out from beneath their trousers.

Almost all clutched attaché cases or briefcases, as if they'd rushed to work and forgotten to dress.

"Clothes can be replaced," said a stiff, gray-haired fellow with green pyjamas and an overflowing briefcase. "But NOT my papers!"

Half an hour after I'd left my room, about a third of the 300 guests had come downstairs. The alarm was still ringing and the receptionist was feverishly hunched over the switchboard.

"Yes, sir! We advise you to come down immediately," he said. "Trouble on the 14th...Yes, ma'am! Trouble on the 14th. Come down now!"

"We had a fire in one room last year," he told me later, with a smile "and the people in the next room wouldn't leave even after the firemen arrived. I guess they didn't want anyone to know they were there."

The longer people took to emerge, the more clothing they wore. One couple looked like they were off to a cocktail party.

"Were you up already?" I asked.

"Oh no," said the woman, who wore makeup and a sequined red blouse. "We just dressed a little faster than usual."

"You put on a tie for a fire?" I said to her husband.

"He always wears a tie," she replied. "In this town, you never know when you might run into the prime minister."

Firetrucks had arrived and teams of firefighters were rushing through the hotel sporting heavy yellow uniforms, pickaxes and oxygen tanks. As they mixed with guests in bathrobes and briefcases, it looked like a strange fireman's ball.

"Twenty-five portable to 27 portable!" crackled a walkie-talkie. "We are on the 14th floor and surveying the rooms... No sign of smoke yet."

Most people were groggy but friendly. I'd been staying there for three days while working in Ottawa, and I hadn't met a soul. But suddenly I knew all my fellow guests. They included a bus tour of senior citizens from Ohio, some vacationing tourists from St. Lambert, Quebec, and a group of American insurance sales reps at a symposium on selling.

The anonymous corridors of our big hotel had been briefly transformed as we traded names, experiences, even addresses. The tiny catastrophe had briefly made us a community, and we all seemed happier for it.

Around 3 a.m., firemen trudged out of the elevator and huddled with the manager. A guest had taken a hot shower and steam had set off the bell. It was a false alarm, and a whiff of disappointment seemed to sweep over the crowd along with relief.

Minutes later, we were packed into the elevators in our rumpled pyjamas, sports jackets and bare feet, exchanging goodbyes like old friends. When I got off at the 10th floor, everyone waved goodbye.

Next morning, the lobby was a different place. Gray-suited men scurried by each other without making eye contact, harried parents shouted at kids to hurry up or they'd miss their plane.

No one said hello to me, and sadly, I didn't say hello back. In truth, I couldn't recognize anyone with their clothing on.

Born to Lose

LOST: One pair cross-country skis.
          Description: Brown. 8-feet long.
          Probable vicinity: Northern Hemisphere.
          Last seen: On feet.

IT'S NOT EASY TO MISPLACE an 8-foot-long pair of skis, but when it comes to losing things, I am never at a loss.

I have been missing pieces of clothing ever since I was old enough to undress myself. I have lost enough gloves and scarves to open a men's fashion shop. I've spent hours searching for my car keys — only to find I can't remember where I put my car.

I was born to lose things.

I realized my skis were missing last month when I was packing up for a ski holiday, and went out to get them on the back balcony. Our frozen hammock was there, along with our buried barbecue and beach chairs — but not my skis.

I looked down in the basement, up in the attic and under the bed. Where the hell were they? I didn't want to rush out and buy new ones, because I wasn't convinced they were really lost.

Accepting that something is officially "lost" is a gradual process, a bit like the five stages of accepting death. For instance, say you're missing your favorite ski sweater. Your thinking goes like this:

Stage 1. Denial: Your sweater isn't really lost. You've just misplaced it. Why buy a new one one? — the old one will show up any day.

Stage 2. Anger: The sweater's been missing a week. You *couldn't* have lost it. Someone must have borrowed it — or stolen it!

You walk the street, eyeing anyone with a sweater vaguely like yours, ready to stop them and say: "Excuse me — but is there a mustard stain under your armpit?"

Stage 3: Depression: You lost it, you *jerk*. Your favorite sweater! What's the matter with you? — You're always losing things!

Why bother to replace it? You'll just lose it again.

Stage 4. Acceptance: Face it. Your sweater is gone. If you don't buy a new one you're going to freeze all winter. Grow up and go shopping.

Stage 5. Resolution: You buy an expensive new sweater. A week later, you take down the ironing board and the old one falls out.

While "losers" like me spend their lives looking for things, other people are "finders," who never misplace a safety pin. This is because they spend their lives devising *systems* to remember where everything is.

They keep their clothing ordered alphabetically and their books arranged by weight. They spend more time organizing their cassettes than they do listening to them.

They have one drawer for striped socks, another for checkered socks and a third for "unidentified patterns." They are always moving things from one drawer to another as the season and their "system" changes. They say things like:

"Don't forget, dear, the winter boots are in the 'current season' drawer and the fall boots are in the 'winter storage' drawer until spring cleaning.

"And I re-arranged the ski equipment. From now on, the ski wax is in with the floor wax."

Just last week, a super-organized friend called me and asked if I had a red hat.

"*You* lost something?" I asked in amazement.

"Don't be silly " she said. "I *found* a red hat in the basement, so I'm calling all the people I know who lose things — like you."

Not surprisingly, I did have a red hat — although I didn't know it was lost until she found it.

Organized friends of mine are always trying to help me devise systems to stop losing things. One friend built me a huge wall system of slots and pockets — a Great Wall of organization.

Two years ago another friend bought me a set of those whistling keychains that beep loudly anytime you whistle at them. The first day I got it I was really impressed. I kept hiding my keys under the sofa, or behind the onion bagels in the freezer, then whistling to see if I could find them.

It was too good to be true , which was confirmed as the days wore on. The keychain didn't just beep when I whistled. It beeped when I hummed, sang, sneezed, coughed, burped, breathed or opened the front door.

After a week of nonstop beeping, I dropped the keychain down a sewer, resigned to the fact I'd rather lose my keys than my mind. And I came to a conclusion: I'd just as soon waste my energy looking for things, as waste it looking for ways to find them.

A Tipple A Day

I WAS DOWN AT A LOCAL BAR recently with a gang of tipsy patrons downing one glass after another, shouting: "To your health!!"

And we meant it. We were celebrating another study on alcohol consumption that found drinking yourself to death can add a few years to your life.

A front-page story had reported: DRINK AT LEAST THREE A DAY — "because drinking in moderation can lessen the chances of heart disease."

The study was the latest in a series of recent victories for health-food haters: we tipplers, gourmets and gluttons who believe that living a long and enjoyable life is not a contradiction.

For more than a decade we've suffered the slings and arrogance of the obsessively healthy: the Perrier-sippers and calorie-counters, the oat-eaters, cholesterol-cultists and granola-gulpers who won't buy tooth paste unless its whole-wheat-flavored and cholesterol-free. People who won't let you drink a beer at their house without going out on the back balcony.

But lately the tide has been turning, as health food icons topple like statues of Lenin. There have been reports:

- That oat bran (yecch) may do little more than it seems to — leave a bad taste in your mouth.

- That several cups of coffee have no harmful effects but — ohh, sweet revenge — de-caffeinated coffee can kill you.

- That the anti-cholesterol craze may create a fat-starved, "mentally-impaired population that lives a few days longer" — in the words of Phil Gold, physician-in-chief at the Montreal General Hospital.

Long-time food villains are being rehabilitated. Eggs, butter, cheese and whole milk — once the Gang of Four of the breakfast table, are again respectable company.

Pasta, the Saddam Hussein of '70s calorie-counters, is now the first choice of the trendy New York dinner host. Even sugar seems poised for a comeback, as Quebec's Jos. Louis Cakes leads a country-wide crusade, guaranteeing all its products as:

"100% Granola Free!"

"Everything that's bad for you will eventually be good for you," predicts my old friend, Hal the Hedonist, a cheerful guy who has been eating and drinking to excess for decades. As we talked, he wolfed down a four-egg salami omelette followed by a shot of brandy and cream.

"Unfashionable food is like out-of-date clothing in your cupboard," said Hal. "If you like it, hang onto it, because eventually it will come back in style. . . Pass the salt please."

Nothing is coming back as fast as booze, said Hal. For years he's been clipping scientific reports that show moderate drinkers have better digestion, lower cholesterol levels and a higher life expectancy than non-drinkers. But this latest study, by no less than the Harvard School of Public Health, amazed even Hal.

It said that two drinks a day can reduce the risk of heart attack by 30 percent. And three to five drinks can cut it by as much as 50 percent.

"*Five* drinks a day!!?" said Hal. "I like to think I can knock a few back, but five-a-day may take more will power than I've got. You need to be some kind of health nut for that."

He was now working on a double-order of fries with mayonnaise, and a side order of BBQ beef jerky.

Hal figures that when the health zealots catch on to the rising benefits of booze, it could take a lot of the fun out of drinking. We'll all have to struggle to keep up.

Government posters will urge: "Five-a-day keeps the doctor away."

Fashionable new-style Health Bars will serve "heavy beer" that gives you a whole day's liquor requirement in one high-octane drink.

Schools will offer adolescents special alcohol supplements in their daily milk: "Guaranteed 3.25% liquor-added." Better-off families will start their kids' morning off with a tall glass of Bailey's Irish Cream.

Meanwhile, non-drinkers will be treated like social lepers.

"Another Perrier, straight up, sir? Why don't I just give you a couple of packs of cigarettes and a cyanide capsule?"

By then, says Hal, other forbidden foods will also be back in fashion. Health freaks will carry personalized salt shakers around their necks, in case restaurants don't offer a "high-sodium menu."

Cereal boxes will say: **"No Bran, Wheat Germ or Other Non-Sugar Additives."**

Coffee will be the health drink of its day. Steamie-and-fry stands will be the rage, after scientists discover that tofu causes cancer.

As health food grows unfashionable, predicts Hal, science will discover that too much exerise benefits no one but physiotherapists and chiropractors. Hospitals will be clogged with victims of jogger's joints, tennis elbow, aerobic knee, walkers' wobble, shrivelled swimskin, Birkenstock back and squash foot.

More studies will find that everyone has only a certain number of breaths to live — and heavy exercising just uses them up faster. People who jogged four hours day will have used most of theirs up and die horribly young, a tragic group, seen as the asbestosis victims of their day.

Hal ordered some more salted peanuts and lifted his glass. "To science!" he said. "This is my fourth drink today — but health is important. Bottoms up."

Still, before you all hoist your glasses, I should remind you that every study has its down side, too. The Harvard report noted that wine-loving Frenchmen have a very low rate of heart disease but a very high rate of cirrhosis of the liver.

In short, a couple of drinks a day will only help you live longer if it doesn't kill you first.

The Write Stuff

I recently read that the U.S. Post Office is trying to teach computers to read handwriting. Apparently postal computers can already read typed envelopes and differentiate between the words:

"215 Brontosaurus Blvd. #334," and "CONGRATULATIONS! YOU'VE JUST WON $1,000,000!"

But so far, computers can't decipher handwritten addresses, so U.S. postal authorities have started a program to train them to analyze thousands of writing styles. In a few years, they say that computers will be able to read *anyone's* writing.

Maybe — but don't bet your ballpoint on it. Before Canadians start investing in similar technology, I thought I'd warn postal authorities what they're up against.

Me.

This may be the age of technology, but there are some frontiers science will never conquer, and my handwriting is one of them. I have been handwriting handicapped, or should I say calligraphy-challenged, since I was old enough to smudge ink. My penmanship is poisoned — with no known cure.

I know this could be a real liability for a writer, like a chef with no taste buds or a florist who is color-blind. But I've always seen it as a challenge — making me a kind of Stevie Wonder of journalism.

If I wrote the autobiography of my childhood it would be called *Years of Writing Dangerously.*

Ever since I first picked up a pencil I've been unable to read what I write. My hand flops over my wrist like a wilted rose. My letters look like they're written by a squirrel with ink on its feet. My B looks like a Z, my M like a V, my Q is just a splotch of blue.

In public school I was teased mercilessly by kids with classy calligraphy.

"Geez, *what* is that — hieroglyphics?" they'd say. Or:

"Ever thought of becoming a doctor. You already write prescriptions."

I still have my old report cards, and my teachers' comments were always the same:

"Josh's handwriting is illegible," said my Grade 1 teacher. "If he does not correct this fault now, he will never succeed at anything."

"I am afraid I must again mention Josh's handwriting," warned my Grade 2 teacher. "He must correct this problem — BEFORE IT IS TOO LATE!"

It already was.

Handwriting had been tough enough when we used large printed letters, but then we switched to "real" writing, where the letters were supposed to somehow *connect*.

Mine always ended up superimposed, one atop the other, and I paid dearly for it. Miss Wilkinson automatically cut my results by 20 marks in every test I wrote — even math, where there were just numbers.

Miss Green looked at my first ink-stained essay and burst into uncontrollable laughter.

Mr. Harding was sure I was using the wrong hand, and made me switch for six months. I was the only person in the history of western education forced to write with his *left* hand.

Miss Jaffe at least understood me. She gave me "U" (unsatisfactory) in handwriting, the lowest mark possible, but "E" (excellent) for effort.

Because I *was* trying. I spent weeks hunched over my desk like a jeweller, trying to form letters someone could read. I took tutorials like "remedial writing" and "handwriting helper." I tried fountain pens and felt pens, mechanical pencils, crayons and even a quill. In high school I was given a fancy pen called the "Diplomat" — that was used to sign the Treaty of Versailles or something.

But if U.S. President Woodrow Wilson's handwriting had looked like mine, World War I would never have officially ended.

I seemed doomed to a career of flipping flapjacks until Mr. Haisman became my Grade 9 teacher. He took three days to decode my first essay, and realized there was a scribe beneath my scrawl.

Soon he got me to type, a one-finger exercise that changed my life. Like the misunderstood hero of *My Left Foot*, my teachers discovered there was a writer hidden beneath my handwriting.

I was no longer a prisoner of my penmanship.

Since then, I type practically everything, from five-word phone messages to birthday cards for friends. When I must write something by hand, I forsake "real writing" and revert to print: fat block-like letters that look like they belong on Sesame Street. I am an adult trapped in the handwriting of a four-year old.

I use my "handwriting" sparingly. I write cheques, which are frequently returned. When travelling, I write only two-word post cards — "HAVING FUN" — though many people think I am referring to a gun.

As a journalist there is an advantage — no one can read my notes — though unfortunately, neither can I.

So forget it, Canada Post. This is one bold American initiative that is doomed to fail. The computer will never be built that can fathom the mysteries of my writing.

To spare you trouble, I've typed this letter, though you probably won't get it because I addressed the envelope by hand. But if I'm wrong, and you do develop a machine that can unscramble my scribble, please let me know.

I've got a whole box of childhood essays, and I'd love to know what they say.

Yours truly,

CHAPTER THREE

City Blights

Battle of the Bagel

IT'S NOT OFTEN I GET A "HOT" SCOOP. So I was thankful for a tip from CBC maven Mark Starowicz. He was flying into Montreal when he met Irving Abella, president of the Canadian Jewish Congress (CJC), clutching a mysterious brown bag.

Ever the newshound, Starowicz asked what he was carrying and reluctantly, Abella revealed his stash: two dozen bagels he was smuggling in for his son in Montreal — from Toronto! — where Abella claimed the best bagels in the world were to be found.

Now, Montreal has suffered a lot of set-backs in recent years, but when the president of the Canadian Jewish Congress is smuggling Toronto bagels into Montreal, our city's reputation is on the line.

The bagel is one of Montreal's "national foods," more popular than poutine, more celebrated than croissant. If Abella was right, Montreal might never recover from the blow. I called the CJC and left Abella a message:

"Urgent: call re bagels."

Then I went out to get some background on my subject.

There is an old Jewish word for legends and myths — "bobbe-mysehs," (literally, "grandmother tales,") — and the origin of the bagel is lost in bobbe-mysehland. Some historians say the first bagel was baked in Vienna in 1683, as a tribute to the king of Poland. It was the shape of a horse's stirrup—a "beugel" in Austrian.

Others say it originated in Cracow, Poland, in 1610, where it was given to pregnant mothers as a good-luck charm and a teething ring. Still others credit Russia or Germany. Whatever the truth, we know that the bagel crossed the ocean about 1900 and settled in New York before migrating North to Montreal.

Like most Montrealers I grew up on the one from the "bagel factory" on St. Viateur — a hole-in-the-wall where people from around the world still line up at midnight for hot bagels. Joe Morena, manager for 30 years, insists the shop's ancient wood ovens give "a smoky, unmatchable St. Viateur street flavor that make us the best bagel factory on earth."

Maybe, but 15 years ago a competitor opened on nearby Fairmount Ave. and challenged the title. Owner Irwin Shlafman claimed his grandfather had *brought* the bagel to Montreal in 1919 and run a bagel shop until 1962 — in the very same Fairmount Ave. building where Shlafman had set up shop.

With the excitement of an archeologist, Shlafman announced he had torn down the building's walls and discovered his grandfather's original wood-burning brick oven, with a petrified bagel still inside. It was irrefutable proof, said Shlafman, that his was the oldest bagel bakery in Montreal — and he promptly named it the Original Fairmount Bagel Factory.

"The secret," he says "is in our dough and our oven. No one makes a better bagel!"

Frankly, the subject is too controversial for me to take sides. Both places now produce about 5 million bagels a year and have helped make the bagel one of the city's best-known foods. Montreal bagels are shipped to dozens of countries and sold at both city airports — along with smoked meat — so parents can give departing children something to remember Montreal.

The anglophone exodus of the 1970s spread decent bagels across Canada, from Vancouver to St. John's, as well as Toronto. And not coincidentally, in the same period, bagels have become an international food sensation.

The U.S. bagel bible, "Bagelmania — The Hole Story," states that the bagel is now found in every North American city, in one out of three restaurants. It has spread from the Bagel Deli in Anchorage, Alaska, to Tokyo, where cinammon-raisin bagels are served up with cream cheese and raw bonito fish.

The book states that Montreal's bagel might be the "best in the world" because of wood-burning ovens that give it a "unique, charred, outer surface."

But greatness has a price. The wood-burning oven is the high-wire act of bagel-baking: Witness the fact that St. Viateur Bagel Factory burnt down in 1984 — a frightening testament to its quality.

Not surprisingly, Toronto bans wood-burning ovens as dangerous. Instead, most Toronto bakeries make an "electric bagel," cooked in a regular oven and so fat you can barely see the hole. In Joe Morena's words: "It's not a bagel — it's a bun."

So, given all this, why was Irving Abella bringing bagels from Toronto to Montreal?

Abella was in town to meet Israeli President Yitzhak Rabin, but understanding the importance of my message, he called back in minutes. Yes, he admitted, he often brought in bagels for his Toronto-born son. They came from a Toronto bakery called Bagel World — a place, Abella declared again, that was home to "the best bagel in the world."

Abella said he brought back Montreal smoked meat in exchange, but I was not to be mollified. What kind of oven did Bagel World have, I demanded: wood-burning or electric?

Abella didn't know.

Suddenly, I was suspicious of his bagel credentials. I said good-bye and called Toronto's Bagel World myself. The owner was an ex-boxer named Joe Zaduk, who had fought in Montreal for years. He'd been in the bagel business 25 years and knew a lot about bagels — the need for a crisp crust, a chewy inside and hand-rolled dough.

But Zaduk quickly admitted he uses a gas-flame oven — and said the only place you can find wood-burning ovens is in Montreal.

"I used to eat bagels in Montreal," he sighed nostalgically. "Now that's a *great* bagel."

"Is yours better?" I asked.

"Well," Zaduk said, "I'd like to think it's as good . . .but better? . . No, I couldn't honestly say that. Montreal's bagel is the standard by which every bagel is compared."

Thank you for your honesty, Mr. Zaduk. As for you, Mr. Abella, you might be an excellent historian and a fine CJC president, but I suspect that growing up in Toronto, you need a bagel appreciation course — and I would be happy to give you one next time you're in town.

To be charitable, I will leave the last word to Joe Morena: "Everyone has different bagel tastes…and I find that the best bagel is always the one you grew up with."

Even if Mr. Abella grew up with the wrong one.

Arctic Chair

IT WAS THE MORNING AFTER the Charlottetown referendum. Canada had said "no" to Quebec and Quebecers had said "no" to Canada — so the advertising brochure seemed strangely appealing.

If you speak English and enjoy fine food, we invite you to help our francophone student waiters and waitresses practice serving customers in English.
        —Institut de Tourisme et d'Hôtellerie du Québec.

The Quebec government's hotel and restaurant training school was desperately seeking anglos for an English-only dinner at its main dining room. Who could say no? I phoned and made reservations.

At 7 p.m. that day, my companion and I showed up for an English après-referendum dinner on St. Denis St. in the heart of French Montreal. We were greeted by a young Québecois maître'd.

"Good even-ing," he said, with a thick French accent.

"Bonsoir," I replied instinctively, then quickly apologized. Like many anglos, I'm used to speaking French in restaurants — partly out of guilt, and partly because it makes food sound better. Somehow, pepper steak never sounds as good to me as "steak au poivre." And "coquille St. Jacques" loses someting as "St. James shell."

But now I was being asked to conquer years of anglo training — and cater to francophones who insisted I speak English.

Ah, Quebec.

We were seated in a large dining room surrounded by tables of anglos, all chatting merrily in English. For a moment, I felt like I was in Toronto.

"Good even-ing", said another man in his mid-twenties, also with a strong accent. "I am Gabriel, your waiter. Would you care for an apéritif?"

Apéritif? Wasn't that a French word?, I thought. But then, what was the English one? Tactfully, I ordered wine.

The service was all in English but the menu was entirely in French, boasting terms to torture any anglo.

Terrine de ris de veau, de homard et de chanterelles. Potage au marmiton. Cuisse de lapin a l'étuvée de chou rouge, sauce aux baies sauvages.

Was this an English dinner, or a French test?

"Please," Gabriel said eagerly. "I will translate the title of each dish."

Soon he was giving colorful English renditions of classical French dishes. "Suprême de canard mariné" became "supreme of marinated duck"— which somehow didn't sound as good.

Le "plat du jour" was "the plate of the day."

And consommé was — consommé.

Some students had English crib cards which they secretly consulted, but Gabriel offered effortless translations, with only the odd lapse.

What is "omble chevalier?" I asked, pointing at the menu.

"Ah, that is a fish!," he said. "In English, I think you call it "Arctic chair."

Yes, I teased him gently, but only when it's served with baked Alaska table.

Into this sea of fractured phrases strode Diana Bruno, the institute's English teacher, ready to correct her students' mistakes. She's heard some great ones — from desserts like "chocolate mouse" and "apple pea" to "vanilla liar cake."

"It's also hard for students to translate nouvelle cuisine terms," she said, "especially since many don't understand them in French.

"What's a sauce 'à la Grenoblaise' or 'à la Lyonnaise?' Who knows that 'laitue chiffonade' is shredded lettuce? When I started this job I didn't know myself."

Over-all, the meal was great and the price reasonable, a gourmet dinner for two for about $40, not including wine. We were sated and Gabriel satisfied by our anglo après-referendum dinner.

"I don't get to practice my English very often," he said as we left. "I moved here from Quebec City and my friends are still all French. I love the mix of languages in Montreal, but I miss a lot because I don't speak English."

Gabriel said he'd like to work in B.C. to improve his English. He was slightly apprehensive because "B.C. voted no in the referendum even stronger than we did, but I'd still love to go if I could find a job."

Our meal ended, and I was reluctant to leave. Outside, shrill voices awaited me on TV: Parizeau, Bouchard, Manning and others eager to tell me that French and English could never get along.

"Bonsoir" I said to Gabriel and the rest of the staff, unable to repress a final French word. And waiter after waiter waved goodbye and shouted a jolly: "Good night."

Festival of the Shadfly

THE FÊTE DE LA ST-JEAN is finally over and the partying can begin. No, not Canada Day —the real festivities.

Don't you know that today is the Festival of Paper in Clermont, Quebec? That the Festival of the Shrimp has just started in Matane?

Are you aware that Thursday is the Festival of the Speckled Trout in Saint-Alexis-des-Monts? And that July 1 is the Festival of Asbestos in Thetford Mines?

We are now at the peak of festival season, the annual period when Quebecers flee their homes in rampaging herds, eager to make up for nine months of cold and confinement.

From the Festival of Milk in Coaticook to the Festival of the Doughnut in St. Malo, from the Festival of the Pig in St. Perpétue to the Festival of the Wood-Burning Stoves in Ste. Julienne, we are celebrating like there was no tomorrow.

And there isn't. The frenzy of festivities is just a symptom of our lives in this giant national freezer, the winter tuque of the planet. Citizens of other countries can spread their lives out over twelve leisurely months. But we are the shadfly of nations, doomed to squeeze all of life's activities into a short burst of summer, all our fun into a few weeks of sun.

We must plant our gardens, renovate our homes, open our summer cottages, take our vacations, move, marry and celebrate our national holidays before the weather turns cold and darkness returns.

The frenzy is most obvious in our festivals, as organizers compete for the 40 odd days a year that are relatively safe from rain, snow, sleet, hail and power blackouts.

The alternative?

Witness poor St. Patrick's Day parade revellers, doomed to struggle like *coureurs de bois* through a blizzard each year, because they foolishly chose March 17 — instead of July 17 — to honor their patron saint.

Better to have followed the example of Knowlton, in Quebec's Eastern Townships, which celebrates an annual midsummer holiday called "Christmas in July." These wise townsfolk take no chances of losing their Christmas holidays to an unexpected December blizzard.

In Montreal, competition for festival locations is particularly intense as organizers battle for a limited number of city streets for an infinite number of festivals —from Carifête and jazzfest to la fête de la St-Jean; from Canada Day, July 1, to Moving Day, also July 1.

Somewhere, there is probably a traffic-control tower holding back eager festivals, like airplanes on a runway:

"Sorry, you can't have Park Ave. for the Festival of Albanian Tree-Climbers this July 6th; it's already reserved for the Kazakhstan Foot-Cloggers Festival.

"But we can let you have University St. on July 20 between midnight and 4 a.m.— once the Festival of Vegetarian Cattle-Raisers is over."

The frenzy to cash in on the sun's warmth extends to our daily lives, too, where our herd-like behavior creates countless unofficial festivities.

They are part of the annual Festival of the Vacation, when 6 million Quebecers take their holiday the same month, closing down the few Montreal businesses that aren't already bankrupt.

Leading the charge is the Festival of Construction Workers, some 100,000 laborers who leave for holiday at exactly the same minute, converge on the Jacques Cartier Bridge all night — then re-converge a day later at the same ten hotels in Ogunquit, Maine.

Hot on their heels is the Festival of the Weekend Cottager — a lemming-like species that plunges onto the Laurentian Autoroute at 4:30 p.m. every Friday, under heavy pressure to have fun in the sun. This desperate creature will stew in four-hour traffic jams, ignore mosquito bites the size of golf balls and leap into lake water so cold it could freeze fish.

All to feel they've gotten the "most" out of summer. The rest of the week, they will join other Quebecers in hovering over the TV to watch the weather channel, following the weekend forecast as if it were a bomb alert.

"Ohmigod! They're calling for showers on Sunday — there goes half the summer!"

And they are right. When you live in a climate like ours, you must squeeze something out of every summer moment, make a festival of every day.

So stop reading this page immediately and go outside. Throw a barbecue for breakfast. Have a Festival of the Club Sandwich at a café-terrace for lunch. Sleep on your balcony, even if it rains.

Eat, drink and be merry, for tomorrow you freeze.

Learning Le French

BONJOUR!

In an attempt to smooth out my subjunctive and perfect my plus-que-parfait, I've recently returned to early anglo adolescent hell. I've registered for a French class.

I've only been at it a couple of weeks, but already I feel like a doomed anglo soul, condemned to re-live the agony of my grade-school past. To start with, there is the challenge of dividing the entire world into two genders, like *la cuillère* and *le couteau*.

Mrs. Spoon and Mr. Knife. Or Mr. Desk and Mrs. Chair. Or Mr. Sun and Mrs. Moon.

Then, there is the maddening mix of personal pronouns as in: "J'aurais dû la lui le leurs les donnes le vendredi." (Whenever in doubt throw in some extra pronouns.)

There are the arcane tenses that you never meet in life, but always meet in books. The conditional future. The imperfect subjunctive. The exterior anterior future posterior.

I am part of the 60 percent of Quebec anglophones who profess to be "bilingue" — but according to my teacher, most of us can't even pronounce the word properly. Over-all, there are two kinds of anglo French-speakers:

ANGLO 1: This person knows all 276 French tenses, and is determined to get them *perfectly* right. Before speaking, he weighs every pronoun, every verb, every word.

Consequently, Anglo 1 never actually speaks French. He spends all his time trying to mentally organize his first sentence. When he does occasionally say something it sounds like this:

"Ah, bonjour Jacques. J'ai — voulu — vous — envoyer — un...ummm...UNE...enveloppe...

"Uh....non. NON! I mean...J'aurais voulu que vous me eus....No, que TU...me eut....Uhhhh... uh...Oyyyyyy."

After several minutes of this, Jacques switches desperately to broken English and Anglo 1 joins him in embarrassed relief, determined not to speak another word until he has finished five more years of intensive French.

He will never change. Francophones will assume Anglo 1 is too arrogant to speak French. In fact, he is just terrified.

ANGLO 2 has a vocabulary of 15 words and one tense, usually the present, and talks like a cave man.

"I am Josh — I live Montreal — I go work— bus — now."

Despite this, he speaks French with the confidence of Molière, filling in the gaps with English words, or going around them with a lengthy verbal detour.

"Ah Jock! Je regarder dans le shopping mall vous player le guitar avec votre drummer…C'est b'en terrifique, là — tabernacle!"

After several minutes Jacques will also switch to English — but Anglo 2 will keep talking "French." Neither party will understand more than half of what the other is saying but they will smile a lot and get along famously.

If Canada has a hope this may be it.

The truth is, until French-immersion schools began to change the anglo genetic code, it was impossible for a native English-speaking Quebecer to completely master French. In the words of one weary woman registering for French class with me:

"There are too many tenses, too many sexes, too many words."

Take the "passé simple" — a tense that was obviously named to taunt anglos, who wonder: "If it's so simple, why can't I understand it?"

In truth, even Francophones secretly call this tense, the "passé pas simple."

As well, no adult anglo can ever master the gender of every word, because they keep adding new ones. And there are few dependable rules.

Why is it Mrs. Suitcase and Mr. Parking lot? How do you know if it's le nintendo or la nintendo? Le perestroika or la glasnost? Who makes up the rules?

And even if you do get them right, you will still be betrayed by your accent. For there are sounds the adult anglo mouth cannot pronounce.

No untutored anglo can say the sound *ueueue*, as in "rue" or "vue." In fact, we can't even write it.

Few of us have fully mastered the guttural "r" in words like "heureux": a sound my *Conversational French* guide recommends you "pronounce far back in your throat, almost as if you were gargling."

Is this a language — or a medical treatment?

Yet as tough as it may be to master French, it's no easier for French Quebecers to conquer English. They wonder why one tooth becomes two teeth, but one booth isn't two beeth. If it is one goose, two geese, why not one moose, two meese?

In the words of the book *Crazy English*, "If we conceive a conception and receive at a reception, why don't we grieve a greption and believe a beleption?"

"I've been studying English my whole life," a frustrated francophone bureaucrat recently told me. "Mais, c'est impossible! — There are no rules. There are only exceptions to the rule."

That's why, whatever your language, I've always felt the best policy is to plunge ahead and fill the air with words. Remember the classic advice offered in the *The Anglo Guide to Survival in Québec*:

"Speaking French badly is better than being silent and correct. If you speak French badly for long enough, you may eventually learn to speak it correctly."

The Sex of Restaurants

THERE IS NO TASK MORE DAUNTING to the average anglo than making a restaurant reservation—the ultimate cultural survival test.

In Ontario, any fool can make a reservation — you just open the phone book and look up your restaurant. But in Quebec, you must first know the *sex* of your restaurant.

Let's say you want a reservation at a little place you heard about from some friends — the Viaduc restaurant.

But is it masculine: le Viaduc? Or feminine: la Viaduc? Or could it be listed under something tricky — like Le Restaurant La Viaduc?

It's not easy to remember your genders when you're standing in a phone booth, in -34°, with your gloves off. And even when you consult your pocket dictionary and find that Viaduc is masculine, your search has just begun.

Is it Restaurant Le Viaduc, or Restaurant du Viaduc? Restaurant les Viaducs, or Restaurant des Viaducs? All are grammatically correct.

It could also be listed under Restaurant Chez Viaduc or Restaurant Chez le Viaduc (over 100 restaurants are listed under Chez alone). Not to mention Restaurant au Viaduc, Restaurant aux Viaducs or Le Restaurant aux Viaducs.

Get one pronoun wrong and you eat at home.

And who's to say the Viaduc is actually classified as a restaurant? It might be listed as a café, and if so, is it a café-restaurant or a restaurant-café?

Or could it be something trendy, like a café-terrace? Each of these have separate listings — hundreds of pages apart.

You don't believe me? Check the Montreal phone book. There are listings for Restaurant-bars and Bar-restaurants. For Restaurant-bistros and Bistro-cafés. There are Restaurant-charcuteries, Restaurant-patisseries, Restaurant-pizzerias and Restaurant-brochetteries.

Not to mention Brochetterie-restaurants.

It's not easy being an anglophone on the telephone. Or afterwards. Because once you've found your restaurant and showed up for your reservation, you still have to order.

Hmmm — now what's the sex of Caesar salad?

Neverendum Referendum

I'VE JUST RECEIVED a copy of a top secret Quebec document prepared by Jacques Parizeau and a team of crack constitutional lawyers. It's the proposed wording for "The Question" to be asked in the PQ's referendum on sovereignty.

In keeping with earlier referenda, it will be a multiple-choice question that keeps all options open. I reproduce the document verbatim:

CLASSIFIED: Quebec government.
SUBJECT: Neverendum referendum.

Welcome to Triple-E referendum: the easy, effective, elective way to create your own country/province/state/kingdom/duchy/rebel enclave/other.

In creating this homeland you may choose among a variety of options. But remember — the country/province/kingdom/etc. you choose is the one in which you have to live.

Which best represents you?
a)Sovereignty
b)Sov/Ass (sovereignty-association)
c)As/Fed (asymmetrical-federalism)
d)Over/fed
e)Under/fed
f)Fed/up

A sovereign Quebec's territory should include:
a)Current borders
b)Current borders, north until St. Sauveur
c)Montreal island, not including the Fairview shopping centre
d) Outremont only

What should be Quebec's national currency?
a)West Island shilling

b)Saguenay centime
c)Laurentian poutinelle
d)Canadian dollar
e)Canadian Tire

Which do you prefer?
a)Triple-E
b)Double-E plus B & B
c)Double-E, plus CBC and NFB, with UIC
d)Single-E with BLT, no GST

Please choose a national animal:
a)Beaver
b)Frog
c)Lamb
d)Black fly
e)Goose
f)Moose
g)Moule (marinière)

Please select a capital city:
a)Quebec
b)Outremont
c)Plattsburgh
d)Fort Lauderdale

What national holiday should we celebrate?
a)Canada Day
b)Moving Day
c)La Fête de la St-Jean
d)La Fête du Homard
e)Good Friday
f) Every Friday

What status should anglo-Quebecers have?
a)Distinct society
b)Indistinct society
c)Extinct society

Which is most important?
a)Social charter
b)Charter of rights
c)Charter bus to Burlington
d)Charcuterie Schwartz

Which of the following should be retained?
a)Complexe Guy Favreau
b)Hydro
c)Big O
d)Loto
e)Train to T.O.

Thank you for participating in the Neverendum Referendum. Unfortunately the country you have requested is not currently available.
Please call back and try again later.
And again.
And again.
And again…

The Hardwhere Store

I CONFESS that when Pascal's Hardware stores first went bankrupt I didn't pay much attention. Like all Montrealers, I'm used to seeing things disappear, often a lot bigger than Pascal's.

There was the Alouettes football team, the *Montreal Star* and Miss Montreal restaurant. There was Ruby Foo's restaurant, Dupuis Frères and Dorchester Blvd. (now boul. René Lévesque).

There were English streets, English signs and the 's in Eaton's. About the only thing in town that refuses to go is the Big O.

Some of these losses seemed important to me, but Pascal's didn't. After all, it was just a hardware store, wasn't it?

So let me come right out and say it: I was wrong. Like a family member whom you don't appreciate till after he's gone, I miss you, Pascal's, more than I ever knew.

You weren't just a hardware store —you were a houseware happening: a Montreal mecca of ordinary odds and ends from lamps to lawnchairs, Pampers to peanuts, plant-holders to plungers.

You were the place I could get everything I couldn't get anywhere else — and now I can't. You were the heart of hardware, with nuts and bolts for dolts like me.

When it comes to hardware, I am a harebrain. I don't know a grommet from a comet, a tisket from a tasket, a gasket from a green-and- yellow basket. And Pascal's was full of people as ignorant as me.

Say I needed a picture hook. At Pascal's I could wander around like I knew what I was doing, examining hampers of assorted hooks till I stumbled on something that looked like it might work.

In a pinch, I'd consult an elderly salesman with a tape measure in his pocket and a pencil behind his ear who had plenty of experience dealing with customers like me.

Salesman: What size picture would that be for, sir?

Me: Uh, it's about *this* big (holding up my hands). It's a Picasso!

Salesman: Ah, a Picasso hook! (reaching into one of 300 bins of picture hooks). Try this — if it doesn't work, bring it back and I'll give you a Matisse hook instead.

It usually worked.

But since Pascal's closed down, I've been left to my own devices. First I tried going to a regular hardware store — only there are almost none left in Montreal, because Pascal's put them all out of business.

So instead I've wound up at an array of home-building supply centres and vast lumberyards where my ignorance is obvious. I find myself wandering aimlessly through giant stacks of plywood sheets and plumbing pipe, searching for the picture-hook section.

Eventually I show up red-faced at the sales counter, where the customer in front of me is holding a pile of blueprints and ordering a Do-It-Yourself-High-Rise-Apartment-Block Kit.

The salesman looks up to see what I want.

Me: Uh, one picture hook, please.

Salesman: Yessir. What kind of wall would that be? Drywall, wet wall, beaverboard, gyproc or rocky road?

Me: Uh, just the kind that goes from the floor to the ceiling.

Salesman: Uh-huh. What about the nails? You want roundhead, flathead or moosehead? Slot-sided or six-sided scruelox? Sheet metal or self-tapping?

Me: What do they tap????

Salesman: Tapped it is, sir. Let's make it a two-inch No. 8 pinhead Robertson sheet-metal self-tapping screw with a No. 13 plaster anchor. Now do you want a drill bit for a 15-16th carboloy rawl plug —or just something simple like a 3/4-inch anchorbolt with a No. 13 self-boring grommet-notching round-awl screwscrapper?

I take whatever he gives me, but it never works, mainly because I can't figure out how to get it into my wall. But I'm too embarrassed to go back and trade it in.

That's why, like many Montrealers, I've been steering clear of buying much hardware since the death of Pascal's — and my home is slowly falling apart.

I need a Velcro thingee for my boot tray, a doodad for the dishwasher and a circuit-stopping something-or-other for the stereo. Every now and then I wander down the deserted block of Park Ave. near Bernard St. where one Pascal's used to be, and peer into the darkened windows hoping to see some sign of life.

But there's no one around except other passers-by like me, staring into the windows in search of someone who can sell them a Picasso hook.

Operation Winter Storm

SNEEZIN'S GREETINGS.

The New Year is here, but looking out my frost-covered window, it's hard to get enthused. A long year of recession, depression and talk of secession has left me and many other Montrealers unprepared for winter. But don't worry. I have a scheme: a daring plan to guarantee every last Montrealer a no-snow winter.

How? We close the island of Montreal and send everyone south till spring. Operation Winter Storm.

Face it, we live in one of the coldest, least hospitable places on earth —a frozen, windswept island that's best suited for beaver, bear and moose. The only reason we stay here in winter is because our parents did, and theirs before them, all the way back to the first settlers.

Only they *had* to stay — their ships were frozen in the harbor. We live in an age of planes, trains and travel agents. We can leave!

Why cling to the primitive customs of the past? Why fight nature for control of the streets? Keeping Montreal, and many other Canadian cities, open for winter is an extravagance we can no longer afford. Here is my plan:

COST ANALYSIS

Closing Montreal for winter would save taxpayers a fortune.

● The City spends $60 million a year on snow-cleaning contracts and hundreds of millions more on snow-clearing equipment. What a waste, when the stuff would disappear on its own if we waited a few months.

Let's sell our snowblowers to a city that can't afford to leave home — like Vladivostok — and use the money to set up a small airline to ferry us to the sun. A mere 9,000 flights and we could evacuate the city's entire 1.8 million people.

"Warm Air" —flying Montreal south for winter.

● The heating bill for my home is $700. Multiply that by the island's 750,000 households and we're looking at a half billion dollars, literally vanishing into thin air. We spend hundreds of millions on winter transit and hundreds of millions more on "winter recreation" — the ultimate oxymoron.

We shovel out skating rinks and carve out ski hills, heat hockey arenas, gymnasiums, museums and libraries — in a desperate effort to amuse ourselves while we hide indoors. Imagine how many Caribbean beach cabanas we could buy for the money. There'd be enough left over to pay everyone a small per diem.

You can't afford to take the time off work, you say?

You already do. You spend most of winter shovelling your walk, scraping your windshield, lacing up your boots and buttoning your coat, all so you can unbutton it later.

Whatever money you make, you spend on winter tuneups and winter tows, winter boots and winter clothes. The truth is you can't afford not to leave.

WHERE WOULD WE GO?

With the money we'd save, we could buy a beach or an island — maybe even a small country. The Turks and Caicos practically begged us to annex them a few years ago, but the cowardly Canadian government refused.

French philosopher Voltaire dismissed Canada as "quelques arpents de neige," but few know he wanted to abandon New France entirely and resettle on the island of Guadeloupe.

"Quelques arpents de sable."

We practically run Florida already — how much more would it cost to buy the whole thing on a time-sharing plan from January to March?

WHAT WOULD HAPPEN TO MONTREAL?

Nothing. When you close down a cottage for winter, you just let the water out of the pipes, lock the door and come back in spring. The same goes for cities. All we have to do is let the water out of the Lachine Canal, put some anti-freeze in the St. Lawrence Seaway and turn off the street lights. Then let winter have Montreal until the snow melts.

Frankly, the city could use the break. There'd be no pollution because there'd be no industry; no wear and tear on the roads because there'd be no traffic; no cracked sidewalks because there'd be no salt.

And when spring came and the snow melted, there'd be no garbage, no orange rinds, no Coke cans and no dog pooh —because there'd be no dogs. Just a well-rested city ready for a well-rested population who'd just be arriving home.

SNOW JOKE.

CHAPTER FOUR

The U.S. and Us

The U.S. and Us

I. AWFUL LAWFUL

Why did the Canadian cross the street?
To get to the middle.

IF YOU SMILED AT THAT JOKE, you are probably a Canadian: a cautious, compromising soul who avoids confrontation. You're also confused. Your country has just turned 127 but it's having an identity crisis, asking adolescent questions undignified for its age:

Who are we? Why are we? What holds us together apart from snow shovels and mosquitoes? Is it all worth it?

Sure it is. From our country's cradle to its modern-day mess, there has been one national purpose, a secret cement that binds Canadians together from sea to frigid sea:

Our subconscious fear of becoming American.

It is the raison d'être behind Confederation, the nightmare behind the Canadian dream. To mark our 127th year I offer a series of stories — one cautious, confused Canadian's attempt to define our national character:

The difference between the U.S. and us.

First, how does the world see us? According to the *Manchester Guardian*: "One Canadian is as boring as three Swiss or five Belgians."

A British survey asked what came to mind when people heard the word Canada and most respondents said: "Rocks."

Al Capone probably best summed up America's feelings when he said: "Canada? I don't even know what street it's on."

We have gotten this image partly because we live next to the world's loudest, most opinionated people, the Disneyland of nations, where everything is larger than life. America's buildings are taller than ours, their food portions are larger and so are their people.

The biggest Canadian flag I ever saw was flying outside a Plattsburgh shopping mall.

But much of our sleepy reputation is well-earned. Unlike our southern neighbor, we have never fought a revolution or a civil war. Few of us have been murdered, mugged or sued. We've had fewer deaths in the making of our country than one week in Los Angeles. We are the Joe Clark of nations: decent but dull, bloodless but boring — exactly as our early ancestors planned.

The birth of a notion: Officially we became a nation in 1867, but our country was really born much earlier — around 1776, the time of the American Revolution. If Americans are descendants of the revolution, Canadians are descendants of the counter-revolution, people with a long and enviable history of playing it safe.

Many of our English-speaking forefathers were United Empire Loyalists, some 50,000 Americans who fled the U.S. revolution. Like good potential Canadians, they heard the sound of gunfire and ran, terrified too much liberty would mean anarchy.

They were evolutionaries: cautious, quiet people scared of too much change — like us.

Worried the U.S. revolution would spread north, these Loyalists teamed up with French Canadian clergymen who were equally scared of revolution — the French Revolution, which was executing people like them.

Many Quebec leaders stayed loyal to France's throne for more than a century after the French Revolution eliminated it. That's why Quebecers kept the fleur-de-lys — the old symbol of Louis XIV and Louis XVI, executed in the revolution.

They haven't flown the fleur-de-lys in France for more than 200 years. Only in Quebec, home of French royalists who joined English loyalists to form a quieter, safer and sleepier country than the one to the south. But what does that make us?

Nebulous nationalists: As revolutionaries, Americans are very patriotic. Every American knows the words to his national anthem, which he sings at baseball games, at barbecues and at bedtime.

As counter-revolutionaries, many of us don't even know all the words to our anthem. We just sing, "We stand on guard, we stand on guard for thee," until the music stops. While Americans are forever pledging allegiance to their flag, we don't talk to flags in this country. It's like talking to mailboxes.

Awful lawful: As revolutionaries, Americans believe in the sacred right to bear arms and use them. Everyone in the U.S. carries a gun:

border guards, subway guards, football guards. In fact, it's easier to get a gun in the U.S. than it is to get medical care.

The U.S. hero is the cowboy, the frontiersman who tamed the wild west. But Canada is probably the only country in the world where our national symbol is a police officer — the Mountie.

Our government sent the Mounties out west before the settlers, to make sure the no-parking signs were up before the horses arrived. The Mountie wears a very Canadian costume: the boots and Stetson of an American cowboy and the scarlet redcoat of a British grenadier. He is a British cowboy, and we generally obey him.

Americans resist authority, from radar patrol to gun control, but we are a law-abiding people who go out of our way to obey the law. Not long ago, in Kingston, a clothing store had a very "Canadian" fire. In the chaos, customers grabbed all the merchandise and rushed out, leaving nothing behind, just like an L.A. riot.

But when the manager chased after the thieves he found everyone waiting politely outside, with the clothing. They had grabbed it to save, not to steal. Nothing was missing — not even a pair of socks. It was quintessentially Canadian: dull but decent, civilized but not sexy, a triumph of the cautious, conscientious, counter-revolutionary values that come with being us.

As my favorite Canadian joke goes:

How do you get 60 drunken Canadians out of a swimming pool?
You say: "OK, everyone — out of the swimming pool."

The U.S. and Us

II. THE LAND OF THE FREEZE

THEY SAY CANADA has only two seasons: winter and July — and this year, even that's pushing it. It is July 19th, but in the Eastern Townships, the leaves are shivering and turning red, as confused as Canadians by a climate that punishes its own.

Foul wind, freezing rain and other (wind-chill) factors have contributed greatly to who Canadians are: a silent, stoic nation of snow-shovelers and salt-spreaders.

We live in a vast, empty land Voltaire dismissed as "quelques arpents de neige." A place the 1877 *European Settlers Guide* described as having "five months of Arctic temperatures and seven months of cold weather." Even our own prime minister, Mackenzie King, lamented that we had "too much geography and not enough history."

Our climate is part of our heritage. If we are quieter, more cautious creatures than our southern neighbors, it is partly because we have spent much of our lives in life's vestibule, dressing to go outside.

We live in the land of the free(ze).

Cautious Canucks: As residents of a warm, sunny land, Americans are an optimistic people: ready to risk a buck to make a buck. They seem cheerful and confident — even when they shouldn't be.

"Why worry? Be happy."

As cold counter-revolutionaries, we are more pessimistic, because we know life's harsh climate can always get worse. Behind every passing cloud is a snowstorm and we have to be ready for it.

As Canadians, we take more life insurance per capita than any other nation in the world. We also save more money. There are 6 million more savings accounts in Canada than there are people.

We are nothing if not cautious, even in how we talk. Ask an American how he is and he'll say: "Great!"

Ask a weather-hardened Canuck and you'll get a more careful answer, in both official languages.

"Not bad ... Pas pire."

"So-so. ... Comme-çi, comme-ça."

"It could be worse."

Unlike our American neighbors we rarely say: "Have a nice day" — because it usually isn't. And what else can we say?:

"Have a damp and rainy day?"

Or "Have an ice one?"

Humble bumblers: From the Persian Gulf war to the congressional floor, America is cocky, decisive and sure of itself. It is always "No. 1."

As Canadians, we are less certain of ourselves — even if the UN says we're No. 1. Part of the reason, I suspect, is that nature has humbled us, intimidated us, overwhelmed us. It has taught us not to boast — even when we should.

Americans love to use superlatives. New York is the "greatest town on Earth." Chicago is the "windiest city on Earth." Boston is the "hub of the universe."

But cross the U.S. border into Canada and superlatives disappear, replaced by qualifiers, like "somewhat" and "possibly."

If Montreal was in the United States, they'd call it the "French capital of America." But we just call it the "second-largest French-speaking city in the world."

If the CN tower was in New York, it would be the "the World's Tallest Tower." But Torontonians bill it as "the world's largest free-standing structure."

Just as British Columbia Place is the "world's largest air-supported domed stadium."

American football teams play in the annual Super Bowl, but what do Canadian teams play?

The Grey Cup. (Yes, it's named after Lord Grey, but if his name had been Lord Super, we'd have named it after someone else.)

No matter what we have, we are never comfortable calling it the biggest or best. Look in the *Guinness Book of World Records* and you'll see that the world's biggest shopping centre is in Edmonton. If it were in Los Angeles, you can be sure it would be called "The World's Largest Shopping Centre: Humunga-mall."

But do Canadians call it that?

No, we call it the "West Edmonton Mall" — just in case the one in East Edmonton is bigger. Behind our bashfulness lurks a sense of frailty and fragility, a fear of being too big for our britches, too cocky for the wilderness and weather about us.

Other countries have ferocious national symbols like the bear, the lion and the eagle. But we prefer the beaver: a chubby, shy, industrious rodent.

Other countries produce movies where the hero survives car crashes, earthquakes and nuclear bombs — so he can make a sequel and survive more.

But not us. From *Bethune* to *Léolo*, Canadian movies never have sequels, because the hero usually dies. Or limps away with frostbite, like the Jesuit priest in *Black Robe*, spared his life only because the Canadian film's director was an Australian.

In this country, you don't play with nature and win.

Even our humor is modest and self-deflating. Americans generally tell jokes that have others as the butt, but as Canadians we are generally the butt of our own jokes — forever destined to lose.

Where does a Canadian end up if he goes to heaven?
At a panel discussion on heaven.

Frankly, I have no problem with any of this. As a typical Canadian, I am content with our national characteristics and cautious about changing them. After all, there is nothing wrong with being the coldest, quietest, most cautious and least cocky country on Earth.

Is there?

The U.S. and Us

III. A NATION, IF NECESSARY

I WAS SITTING at a busy New York café a few months ago when a young woman approached my table.

"Excuse me," she said. "I hate to be so bold, but could I possibly ask you what you're eating, if you don't mind my asking." In a flash, I knew — she was Canadian! — and I said so.

"Gee!" she said. "How did you guess?"

Because no one but a Canadian could have asked such a convoluted question. A Parisienne would simply have eyed my meal in admiration — or disdain.

An American would have said: "Any good?," and scooped a bite off my plate. But only a Canadian could create such a timid, tortuous sentence, so dense you could never take offense, so sweet you could fall asleep.

We are a nation of diplomats, the world's most polite people, trained from childhood to apologize before we speak. Nothing distinguishes Canadians from our American neighbours more than our quest for compromise, our relentless search for safe, middle ground.

Bump into an American and he will usually say something straightforward like: "Hey! Watch it, buddy."

But bump into a Canadian and he will always say the same thing: "I'm sorry."

Then you'll say: "No, I'm sorry!" and he'll say: "No, I'm sorry!"— apologizing back and forth till you're both exhausted. As Canadians we will talk forever, because we are too polite to say what we mean.

Take our constitutional quarrel (I wish someone would), where there were no real statesmen or memorable speeches. Joe Clark, the Nembutal of nation-builders and Robert Bourassa, the zen master of Confused Federalism, both spoke in sentences of such mind-numbing tedium no one knew what they wanted — including them.

Instead of a civil war, we waged a civil bore.

It's been like that throughout our history. Other nations celebrate battles, wars and revolutions. But Canadians celebrate only one date: 1867 — Confederation — a series of meetings. And we've been meeting ever since, addressing our major differences by avoiding them.

Former Canadian prime minister MacKenzie King faced a political crisis similar to ours, during World War II. English Canada wanted conscription and French Canada didn't, so King found a classic Canadian compromise.

He held an endless two-year debate on conscription and didn't bring it in until the war was almost over, earning himself a place as one of our great complacent statesmen. As Canadian writer Eric Nicols observed in a light-hearted look at Canada back in 1967:

U.S. President Franklin Roosevelt said: "We have nothing to fear but fear itself."

John F. Kennedy said: "Ask not what your country can do for you, but what you can do for your country."

MacKenzie King said: "Conscription if necessary, but not necessarily conscription,"—as confusingly Canadian a statement as ever was spoken.

Imagine how leaders of other times might have re-phrased their famous statements if they had been Canadian, said Nicols. For instance:

Julius Caesar, crossing the Rubicon: "The die is cast, but I don't believe in gambling."

Or Horace Greeley: "Go west, young man! Or east. Or north-by-east. Or south-by-west. Or ..."

Or Winston Churchill, addressing England in 1940: "We shall fight on the beaches, possibly ... We shall fight on the landing grounds if necessary ... We shall never surrender, unless there is no alternative."

Compromise and convolution are the essence of being Canadian, one of the few things we do as well as anyone on earth. We stall. We study. We delay. We dilute. We distract. We do anything to avoid doing something.

If Boris Yeltsin was Canadian, he would never have stood on a tank. He'd have sat on a task force.

In the words of the very Canadian commander of United Nations forces in former Yugoslavia, Maj.-Gen. Lewis W. MacKenzie:

"If Bosnians were Canadians we'd simply take the whole population and bore them to death with conferences. I used to hate all the endless political talk at home. Now, I can hardly wait to get back to it."

Well-said, sir. Like you, I do not mind our preference for words over weapons. With luck, we will eventually use many of them to solve our political problems — working out a compromise so equitable, so complex and so Canadian no one understands it.

"A nation if necessary, but not necessarily a nation."

Our history of hesitation has served us well. When our cautious English and French forefathers decided not to join the American revolution two centuries ago, they couldn't have hoped for better results.

Sure, we often feel threatened by the pizzazz and panache of our colorful southern neighbor, but I think America should feel threatened by us. Our country's existence suggests the American Revolution was an utter waste of time, a lot of blood spilled for nothing, when a couple of centuries of meetings and constitutional conferences could have cleared things up without firing a shot.

If George Washington had fought a little less, and talked a little more, maybe the U.S. could have avoided its revolution altogether — and slowly, cautiously and quietly built a kinder and gentler America.

Like us.

Mad About Metric

I READ that the Canadian government has spent $45,000 on a kilogram of metal — and it finally got exactly what it paid for.

The lump of metal is Canada's "official" new kilogram, a precisely calibrated weight, purchased in Europe to test the accuracy of all Canadian scales. Thank goodness someone in this country will finally know what a kilogram weighs, because anything metric is a mystery to me.

Take those police Info-crime bulletins:

"Wanted: male, brown hair.

"Height: 1.78 metres. Weight 68 kg."

I have no idea what size this person is — whether he's as big as a professional basketball player or as small as a ballerina. He could be my brother — and I wouldn't know.

It's been 20 years since we introduced the metric system and I still haven't adapted. Show me a metre and I still see a yard, give me a kilometre and I'll take a mile.

The sad truth is that most adult Canadians are as lost as me. Admit it: How many of you know your height in centimetres, or your weight in kilograms? My driver's licence identifies me as a "1.83 metre, 88 kg." object.

As far as I'm concerned, I sound like an enormous piece of cheddar cheese.

We live in a country where almost no one over 30 knows how fast they are driving, or how much coffee they are buying , or how cold it is outside.

We spend our lives in a mathematical twilight zone, converting everything we see and do: multiplying kilometres by 0.6., and temperature by $9/5 C + 32$.

Or is it vice-versa?

I don't even know my body temperature anymore. I grew up thinking 98.6 degrees meant "normal" and 102 meant: "call the doctor."

Now, "normal" is about 37° C (I think). But when I hear that number, I sound very sick — maybe even dead.

Nothing in life is easy for a metric misfit like me. I hear the weather forecast but I don't know the weather until I look outside.

25 cm. of snow? — sounds like an avalanche. After a childhood spent basking in 90-degree temperatures, 30°C makes me think dufflecoat, not swimsuit.

For Quebec anglos like me, it can be even more exhausting, since we must often translate quantities before we convert them. Have you ever tried listening to the weather in French while converting to Farenheit in English?

"La température aujourd'hui est 26 degrés avec douze centimètres de précipitation et des vents de 35 kilomètres par heure."

Sure.

And these are the easy metric measurements. My electricity bill is now listed in "kilowatt-hours" and my tire pressure in "kilopascals per centimetre" — easy to understand if you're a physicist.

Land is measured in hectares, which are equal to 2.47 acres — though unfortunately, I never figured out what those were, either. I spend half my life translating from metric to imperial and then back again.

Sales clerk: This piece of cheese is 750 gm. Is that enough?

Me: Uhh, let's see, 750 times .6 is about 42, or is it 4200? — Geez I dunno — just make it 5 grams of cheese, OK?

Maybe some day it will all be worth it. We will live in a logical, rational society where every citizen knows how many kilowatts there are in a hectare, how many centimeters there are in a kilogram, how many cubits are in an ark.

But in the meantime, how much of our nation's mental energy is wasted on converting and calculating? How many work days are lost, how many kilopascals — sorry — joules of mental energy are burned?

Even when you finish calculating the size of your steak, you must still calculate the price, since no one knows what anything costs any more, now that we added the GST.

Get a haircut and you need a math degree to work out the final price:

One trim: $12.65 x 7% GST + 6.5% percent PST

Times 9/5 C + 32.

The government can buy its official kilogram — along with an official metre, an official hectare and an official degree Celsius. Some day they will probably buy a metric hour as well, divided into 10 metric minutes and 10 deci-secs.

But it will be too late for me. I am a relic of the old Imperial system, all 193 pounds of me. I will walk my final mile. I will struggle for my last ounce of breath. I will never go metric.

I will fight to the last 2.5 centimetres. Plus GST.

How's Your Constitution?

"QUESTIONS ABOUT THE FUTURE OF CANADA?" the ad in the paper asked.

Well, who doesn't have them these days? I decided to phone the ad's toll-free number and get the answers.

"Government of Canada," a cheerful young man said. "Gouvernement du Canada."

"Hi! I was wondering about Canada's future," I said. "Do you think it has one?"

"That depends on you," he replied. "Let me send you some information."

"Like what?" I said.

"Well, we'll start with a 60-page copy of the new constitutional proposals, as well as a copy of the 'detailed proposals.'

"We'll also include a study of the European common-market model, a special task force report on aboriginal issues and a report on the Canadian identity."

Suddenly the phone felt very heavy in my hand. My chest constricted and my constitutional life flashed before me. I had a fleeting desire to move someplace more simple — like the rebel Soviet enclave of Chechnya.

I was having a constitutional attack, but the young man was still talking.

"We'll also be including a study on economic union, sir, along with a history of Canada's constitutional negotiations and a speech by the prime minister!

"Then, once you've read everything, we'd welcome a letter from you saying what *you* think!"

Face it, it's not much fun to be a Canadian these days. Not only must you put up with snowstorms, recession, depression and February, but you must also be a part-time constitutional lawyer, with the fate of the nation resting on your shoulders.

If you're an English Canadian you must know the entire history of constitutional reform, from the Quebec Act of 1774 to the Lindros Affair of 1991.

You must understand why Quebec is distinct — rather than unique, special, unusual, particular, peculiar, atypically singular or eccentric — and why you're not.

If you're a French Quebecer you must understand why Westerners want five senators for every three people, and why they go berserk at the sight of a bilingual cereal box.

No matter who you are, you must be ready to be consulted, because the people elected to lead you are determined to follow you. Like a terminal patient in a hospital, you must have your vital signs checked and your polls taken every day.

"Sorry, sir, your constitution is failing fast! I'd recommend a bypass on the 401, maybe even a living transplant to Scarborough."

Committees have already interviewed every man, woman and moose in the land, from the Newfoundland wheat farmer to the Manitoba fishermen. Where will they go next — nursery schools? Pet shops? Cemeteries?

How did it come to this? When I was young it was easy to be a Canadian, part of a compromising nation that usually muddled its way ever forward toward the middle.

Sure, you had to sing "God Save the Queen" and "O Canada!" but in exchange you got medicare, gun control and the right to shop in the U.S. on long weekends.

We were bland, boring, colonial — but content.

The trouble started when our politicians decided to make us exciting and bring home the constitution, a strange object that arrived on our shores like an alien virus. Like something out of a horror film, it leaped off the ship and began to terrorize the land.

The Curse of the Constitution!

The horror of the amending formula! The mystery of the distinct-society clause!

"Canada! A cast of 27 million! See it while it lasts."

Ever since, there has been hell to pay: rising tempers, sinking morale and growing intolerance. We want to be consulted but not be involved, to keep our country together but not to compromise.

Somehow we have lost sight of the middle. We are a nation under siege —by ourselves. I am afraid the time has come to face the fact there is no solution to the constitution. It is too dangerous to be left in

Canadian hands.

I'm not suggesting we give up on Canada but rather that we rediscover it. Let's settle our differences as we always did —by ignoring them.

Let's send the constitution back to England, guarded by experts in consultation fatigue and other forms of toxic democracy. There, it should be sealed in a large lead box and buried far beneath the Earth's surface, with a huge warning:

DEADLY CONSTITUTIONAL WASTE.
DO NOT OPEN AGAIN!

Constitutional Knock-Out

WARNING: This column contains hazardous constitutional
material. May cause drowsiness, dizziness and nausea.

I WAS AT A DINNER PARTY last week when the conversation-killer came
up — the constitution.

The hostess protested, saying it was a tedious topic, unfit for public
gatherings, a sure-fire party-pooper. But it was too late. The debate had
started and the results were swift and deadly: one guest fell asleep in
his chair as if he'd been hit with a lead pipe; a second and third soon
followed, and within a half-hour, the hostess had gone to sleep.

Hmmm, I thought, surveying the now-empty room: this is powerful
stuff, a toxic constitutional substance that can silence critics, disperse
crowds, probably knock out a bull elephant. In fact, the mere mention
of the word constitution probably has you turning to the next page —
if you haven't already.

But think again. Canadians invented frozen fish, the foghorn and table
hockey, and managed to market them all. It's time we found something
useful to do with our constitutional debate. Here are some suggestions:

A sleeping aid: Insomniacs like me try all kinds of desperate ways to
lull our minds to sleep. We listen to tapes of waves, waterfalls and
windmills; birds, bees and swaying trees. Yet all these sounds are
positively exciting compared to the drone of a first ministers' conference
or a constitutional briefing. Why not market them? Imagine a tape of:

The Complete Speeches of Joe Clark.

A Variety of Vacillations, by Robert Bourassa.

Mes Rocheuses!, by Jean Chrétien.

My Most Humiliating Moments, by Lucien Bouchard.

My eyes get heavy just thinking about it.

A sports strategy: While watching the Olympics, I couldn't help
thinking that our constitution could be used to slow down opponents,
like a "stall" play in basketball or "ragging the puck" in hockey.

How fast would the U.S. Olympic basketball "Dream Team" move if it had a Triple-E defence chasing it down the floor: a squad of Canadians reciting Senate weighting formulas "requiring seven provinces with 50 percent for constitutional reform, 6.5 provinces with 38.4 percent for reform of reform ..."

The Americans' eyes would glaze over so fast they'd be lucky to see the basket, let alone hit it with a jump shot.

Punishment: Studies show the word "constitution" produces fatigue and misery in any Canadian from eight to eighty. This could be put to positive use:

●If your kids are acting up, threaten to show them a disciplinary video of MeechMusic — and see how fast they straighten out.

"No dad — Not THAT!!!! — Ple-e-eease. Why can't you just lock me in my room for three days instead?"

● Prison officials already subject prisoners to techniques like the "pink room," a bright pink jail cell said to cool out aggressive inmates. Why not try locking them in a "constitution room" instead? Imagine a solitary cell with nothing but the voice of Clyde Wells debating say, Jacques Parizeau, from morning to night?

Amnesty International would probably complain it was inhumane treatment.

National security: The *Calgary Sun* recently ran a cartoon that showed a squad of riot police dispersing a crowd, by reading constitutional amendments, instead of using tear gas.

Good idea. Next time there's trouble at the Mercier Bridge, let's keep the Quebec provincial police away and call in someone to broadcast the terms of "aboriginal self-government" as it pertains to "inherent rights."

The bridge would be empty in 15 minutes.

Foreign affairs: If it works on Canadians, maybe the constitution could have a similar effect on foreigners, if we translated it. Let's send a squad of Canadian peacekeepers armed to the teeth with constitutional clauses to move through Yugoslavia with loudspeakers, reading stuff like:

"Bosnia constitutes, after Serbia, a distinct society that includes a unique culture and a civil-law tradition. Yugoslavians are committed to the vitality and development of official language minorities, the inherent right to indexed senatorial salaries and ...."

It would be the fastest ceasefire in history: all of Sarajevo would soon be asleep. If it worked in Yugoslavia, we could translate our constitutional weaponry into other languages and send it off to trouble spots around the world, from Sri Lanka to Los Angeles.

Wear them down with Concentrated Meech. Scare them with Allaire. Sock 'em with Spicer and mop up with Beaudoin-Dobbie and a volley of Triple-E. Toss in the threat of a referendum and no country in the world could hold up. They'd be worn out, wasted and so eager to return to normal life they'd be ready to sign anything.

Like most Canadians.

Common Law Country

I'VE COME TO THE CONCLUSION that constitutions are like marriage contracts. They are easy to sign before the wedding, when both parties are rosily optimistic about their future.

But they're tough to renegotiate once you've lived together a while.

Our country has spent the last ten years writing up a new set of vows, that both sides will probably refuse to sign. It's really quite understandable — the mistake was thinking we could re-write our marriage contract in the first place.

Imagine trying to spell out the unspoken rules of your marriage after ten years with your partner.

"OK, Honey, I do the dishes and you make dinner, except on Tuesdays and Thursdays when I have the kids because you do aerobics. Write that down."

"Yeah, but I take classes Wednesdays, so you have to do dinner and car pool until summer. Put that in the agreement, too."

"Wait a minute — I want a veto over any major schedule change."

"Why? I have my own distinct needs. I want a veto, too!"

Pretty soon you'd start to forget your relationship was actually pretty good before you tried putting it in writing.

As Canadians we have unwritten agreements that go back a national lifetime and part of the deal is we don't talk about them.

Canadians know Quebec is distinct, in language, culture and other ways, even if they can't stand to put it in writing.

And Quebecers know they have done well by Canada — even if they're so proud they'll separate from Canada before admitting it.

If the accord is defeated this Monday, I don't believe we will ever see another constitutional agreement signed by all ten provinces. I suspect that for as long as we remain a country, we will have an unsigned constitution — like an unfinished symphony — but who says that can't be beautiful?

I've been to awful countries that had wonderful constitutions, like the former Soviet Union. And I've been to countries, like England, that don't have a constitution at all.

Just because we're too old to go back to the altar and renew our vows, doesn't mean we can't live well together. We can still have a common-law relationship, share bed and breakfast, and work out our problems one by one, from French language and aboriginal questions to unemployment and women's rights.

If we get over the tension of the next few months, maybe we can eventually get back into our old routine and forget our current spat. We could probably get along fine for another 125 years.

In the meantime, if you feel a bit depressed when you wake up and read the results Tuesday morning, follow editorial cartoonist Aislin's immortal 1976 advice:

"Take a Valium."

And whatever happens, I'll be here next week, if you will.

Border Disorder

IT WAS THE END OF MY WEEK-LONG VACATION in New England and the Canadian customs officer was staring at me with X-ray eyes.

"Anything to declare?" he asked, peering through my car window.

"Nope, nothing at all," I said smugly. His eyes flickered with suspicion — I could practically hear him thinking:

"SEVEN DAYS in the U.S. and *no* purchases…Sure, buddy, next thing you'll be telling me you didn't even gas up."

Minutes later he was ransacking my car. He tore through suitcases, sniffed at T-shirts to see if they'd been worn, studied my old tennis racquet to make sure I hadn't bought a new one and scraped it up with sandpaper.

But he didn't even find a U.S. toothpick. Little did he know I am at the cusp of a hot new shopping trend: Canadian cross-border shoppers who are crossing back into Canada. Here is my story.

Like most Canadians, I've been dabbling in the shop'n'smuggle trade since I was old enough to wear clothing. I know all the Canadian techniques to slip stuff back over the border: Rub mud on your new sneakers, soak your jeans in the tub to make them look faded, burn all sales receipts and top up the tank at the last gas station before the Canadian border.

My sporadic shop'n'smuggle episodes reached fever pitch a few years ago with the introduction of the GST (Go South Today). Like millions of Canadians, I rebelled with my feet and stopped shopping in my own country.

I began to purchase my polo shirts in Plattsburgh and my wine in Winooski. I drove 100 miles to fill up on cheap American gas that I burnt up driving home.

In my search for sales, I started to pile up things I didn't even need: a sleeping bag I never slept in, a short-wave radio I never listened to, a "dual-bladed radish slicer and dicer."

And I hate radishes.

My frenzy was fed by mushrooming American factory outlets — bizarre discount-shoping villages set up only to trap GST-weary

Canadians.

Call any dingy U.S. store a "factory outlet" and instantly it fills with Canadians, salivating like Pavlovian dogs, including me. I've always hated shopping, but somehow these places cast a strange spell over me — a crazed desire to buy anything that doesn't include GST.

"Geez, a fluorescent green sock-and-suspender set for only $17.99. It'd cost *at least* $18.99 back home." So what if a shoe didn't fit or a shirt was the wrong color? I'd buy it anyway, as long as it was on sale. So what if I had to fight off 500 crazed Canadians battling their way through bins of clothing? It just added to the excitement of the event: competitive shopping, featuring more elbows than NHL hockey, more brand names than the Olympics.

Last year, I visited two of the great shrines of New England shopping: North Conway, N.H., and Freeport, Me., entire towns of factory outlets that have no apparent residents apart from 24-hour banking machines.

Conway is set amidst the majestic White Mountains and Freeport is near the sea, but like every tourist there, all I remember are the mountains of bargains, the sea of "sale" signs and a wallet as empty as the feeling in my soul.

In retrospect, I was an anti-GST junkie, a crossborder-shopping addict whose problems were starting to show. My house was filled with clothing that didn't fit and electronics that didn't function, and I couldn't give anything back because the stores were 200 miles away.

Worse, most of the merchandise turned out to be for sale in Montreal stores too, stores that were going bust while U.S. stores boomed. I talked to friends going through similar shopping crises and we shared our experiences in a growing support group of Cross-Border Shoppers Anonymous, that slowly helped me lick my habit.

Two weeks ago, I went to the States for the first time in four months, shopping for something new — a quiet outdoor vacation. I was as nervous as an ex-alcoholic entering his first bar. Could I face an all-out sale?

To my amazement I didn't even get the shakes. For days, I barely glanced at U.S. store windows, and when I did, the sales didn't seem as spectacular or the merchandise as good as I remembered.

The thrill was gone.

For six days, I went cold turkey. I didn't even enter a store until the trip home took us through North Conway and an hour-long traffic jam of Canadian cars double-parked outside a crush of discount stores.

When we passed a "super sneaker sale," I couldn't resist a peek. Inside, it was as ugly as a bread riot in Moscow. Shoe boxes were strewn about the floor and hundreds of people were tearing through them, battling over the last Size 7.

Amid the madness, I somehow found myself holding a pair of pump tennis sneakers at one-third the retail price!! — and suddenly I could feel my stomach churning.

True, I'd just bought a pair of tennis sneakers in Montreal that would probably last me years. True, I hated the pump look — but they were so cheap, how could I afford *not* to buy them?

Maybe I'd buy a pair and keep them in the closet for a year, I thought. Maybe I'd even get two pairs to last me through the decade.

And how about the great deal on "cross-trainer sneakers" — whatever they were — and the sale on mountain-climbing sneakers, in case I ever started climbing mountains? And what about the ...

Suddenly I felt a hand on my shoulder. It was my Significant Other Shopper, and she looked concerned.

"Snap out of it," she said. "You already have four pairs of sneakers at home."

She grabbed my hand and we fled for the car and the border. Anyone out there need a radish slicer?

The Gull War

II. RETURN OF ATTILA

I'VE DECIDED that after a nuclear war, the cockroach will not inherit the earth. It won't stand a chance against the pigeon.

Earlier I described my running battle with a nasty gang of birds who had taken over my house, and turned my back balcony into a pigeon motel, pooping on my balcony and cooing outside my bedroom window at 4:30 a.m.

No matter how often I chased them off, they always returned "home."

I thought I'd solved the problem by wrapping the back of my house in thin piano wire, turning my home into a prison. Unfortunately, it was only minimum security.

All that week, the pigeons hovered by the wiring, flapping and beating their wings in a frenzy until they squeezed their way inside. Their leader, a fat, aggressive bird I call Attila, kept bouncing on the wires as if they were trampolines. Within a few days, half the wiring had snapped.

My balcony looked like the scene of a jailbreak, with a dozen noisy jailbirds happily ensconced in a new nest. I could almost admire them for their determination.

Almost.

I kicked the nest off and took new measures. Since my last pigeon dispatch, I've received advice from dozens of people, each battling their own flock:

Mrs. Greenblatt, a sweet-sounding older woman, suggested I poison them with Raid.

Mrs. Vos, 80, recommended mothballs — "they hate the stuff." Mrs. Zabinsky has fought a 30-year pigeon war and only recently claimed victory, with the help of an exterminator.

"The secret is Vaseline," she said, with certainty. "Smear your balcony in Vaseline, and I guarantee they'll be gone in a day."

What could I lose?

Yesterday, my brother Mike went out and caked the entire back balcony in a giant vat of Vaseline.

The result? The pigeons skid around on the Vaseline, but look like they're having fun, especially when they leap over the mothballs, like skaters doing barrel jumps. I have built an amusement park for birds — Josh's Pigeon World.

Meanwhile, Attila monitors my every movement from the neighbor's roof. I can practically hear him discussing the situation with his pal, Genghis:

Attila: Geez, the bald guy still won't give up. He's a tough old bird — a real pest.

Genghis: Yeah, human beings are tough to train. They're like cockroaches — nothing gets rid of them.

Today, I sought professional advice. Macdonald College's raptor centre just faxed me a sheaf of "humane, ecological solutions" to the pigeon problem.

For instance, I can play recordings of "bird distress calls." This will upset the pigeons and eventually drive them away, if I don't mind the sound of birds being strangled, eaten and drowned on my balcony, 24 hours a day, for the next few months.

I also tracked down the city's leading pigeon expert, a man who calls himself "Monsieur Pigeon." He was a chartered accountant until six years ago, when he got involved in a friend's pigeon problem.

Today, he is Montreal's chief pigeon-buster, waging war against them everywhere from the city's museums to the casino.

"Pinwheels, fake owls and snakes, Vaseline, bird calls — everyone thinks they have a solution," said Monsieur Pigeon. "But nothing works for long. The only solution is to seal off your balcony in bird netting."

Net my balcony?

Uh, I think I'll give the vaseline and mothballs a few more days. But just in case, my brother is out buying 1500 square feet of pigeon netting. It's tough, black mesh, the maximum-security wire of the pigeon world, and strong enough to catch a shark.

But is it tough enough to keep out Attila?

My friends are all rooting for me, but my next-door neighbor seems delighted by my dilemma. A soft-spoken, gentle fellow, he was locked in a five-year battle with some mean pigeons, but a few months ago, they disappeared.

"I'd always wondered where they'd gone until I read your column," he said the other day. "Congratulations! You've got my flock!"

Well, how had he managed to chase them away? I asked.

He smiled strangely. It turns out he had borrowed a .22-calibre rifle and "picked them off" from the roof at night.

"You shot pigeons in the middle of the city!" I said. "That's awful!"

"Yeah," he said, with a strange smile of satisfaction. "I thought so, too…Would you like to borrow the rifle?"

Not yet, I said. Not yet.

CHAPTER FIVE

Away in L.A.

Why Not Worry?

LOS ANGLELES— I was flying into Los Angeles and the flight attendant was explaining the usual emergency routine, but her words were clearly Californian.

"Now remember, folks," she chirped over the intercom, "if the cabin pressure drops, an oxygen mask will fall into your lap.

"After you're finished screaming, place the mask firmly over your mouth — and unlike President Clinton: Inhale!"

It was a fitting start to my winter in California, a place where everyone has a smile on their face, and strangers tell you to "have a great day," because a nice one isn't good enough.

I've only been here six weeks and I'm already on a first-name basis with all kinds of people — from the woman who sold me movie tickets last night to a cop who gave me a parking ticket. I've been chatted up by grocers, plumbers, gardeners and car mechanics; I know more about Jerry, my mailman, than I do about some of my oldest friends.

Los Angelenos might have drive-by shootings, gang warfare, muggings, murders and riots, but they sure are friendly. The informality starts at first encounter, when every living soul insists on telling you their first name, from the long-distance operator to other professionals.

"Good evening. I'm Gerry, and I'll be your heart surgeon today. Have a good bypass!"

Like most respectful Canadians, I was brought up to call people Mr. or Ms., especially when I don't know them. But in the U.S., using someone's second name is considered phony and pretentious, like calling someone "your lordship."

Typical are waiters, required by California law to give their name and acting credits before they hand you a menu. Then they sit right down at your table to discuss your meal:

"Hi, I'm Marty. How are you folks doing tonight?

"This evening I'd recommend the fresh kiwi seaweed burger with jalapeño ahi ahi butter and sun-dried Malibu tofu paté."

Worse, they force *me* to participate in these rituals. I recently rented a TV and actually had the following phone conversation:

- Hi! Colortyme Rentals. This is Shannon speaking. What's *your* name, please?

- Uh, Mr. Freed. Do you rent TVs?

- You bet, but I'm afraid I need your *first* name.

- *(Sigh)* It's Josh.

- Great! I'll just put your name down in our file, and pass you on to Buddy, who's in charge of TVs. It's been nice talking to you, Josh!

Seconds later, there was another voice:

- Hi! This is Buddy! Who's speaking, please?

- (Between gritted teeth): Josh.

- Josh! Shannon's been telling me all about you. . . . How're ya doin' today?

Why does this experience make me want to scream? Why do I find it so difficult to tell everyone in Los Angeles my name? By Canadian standards I'm a fairly informal, friendly person, but here in L.A., I feel like a grouch, as stodgy as the butler from *Remains of the Day*.

I cannot bring myself to say "How're ya doin'?" I choke on the words: "Have a nice day!"

I am the only person in California who hears someone say "Thank you," and replies "You're welcome."

Everyone else says: "For sure."

Or: "You bet."

What is wrong with me? — or is it them? Are Canadians a nation of grumps and grouches — or do Californians suffer from terminal good cheer?

Why must they always BE HAPPY? Why *not* worry? — at least a little?

Some of the difference is probably just the weather. It's easy to ask "How're ya doin'?" when the sun is always shining. Easy to wander out and say "Hi!" to the mailman when you don't need boots and three layers of clothing to get to him.

But I suspect most of the difference between our countries is explained by history. Canadians inherited their formality from England and France, orderly societies with a place for everyone and everyone in their place. Many French Quebecers still call even acquaintances "Madame" or "Monsieur," out of old-fashioned respect. The U.S. prefers to think of itself as a classless society, where you're on a first-name basis with every one of your "fellow" Americans.

You can call your favorite superstar Michael, your talk-show host Arsenio, your first lady Hillary. You feel like Jackie and Bo and Roseanne are old friends.

So what if they make a million bucks a year and you make a few thousand? So what if they live in Beverly Hills and you live in South Central? So what if you can't walk in their neighborhood and they can't walk in yours?

At least you're all friends.

Alien Rights

LOS ANGELES—Yesterday I found myself facing one of those momentous L.A. decisions, where every little choice has huge repercussions.

I had to order a hamburger.

Did I want a chicken hamburger, a beef hamburger or a "fat-free turkeyburger?" the counter man asked, beginning the usual California quiz. "How about our new garden burger? It's 100-percent meat-free!"

Would that be with avocado-and-Chinese-mushroom topping or with Danish-mozzarella-and-spicy-meatballs? On a whole-grain sesame roll — or sourdough pita?

And what about my side-salad dressing? Did I prefer lemon-honey-mustard, or Cajun barbecue, or avocado-and-goat-cheese or — but my eyes had glazed over.

"You make the decision!" I wanted to scream, but I knew it would be considered an un-American activity. He would suspect me of being Canadian, or worse — an "alien," as they officially call us here.

I suppose I am. Having an endless number of choices is a strangely American symbol of liberty, in a land where freedom is measured by how many kinds of dressing you can get with your salad. You can order your yogurt lite, super-lite, low-fat, fat-free, totally fat-free, or no-cholesterol. You can get your coffee regular, decaf, half-caf, double-decaf and espresso decaf in sizes like "short," "tall" or "Grande."

Ordering is a language unto itself: i.e., "Gimme an extra-large half-caf-decaf cappuccino, with half-and-half and low-cal brown sugar."

Here in the land of the individual, having lots of choice is more important than what the choices are. As Miss Piggy might say:

"Having more choice means having more."

Or does it?

To this Canadian, the staggering choice available here is sometimes exhausting, partly because many choices lead to the same place. There are 100 kinds of cheese at my cheese counter, but every one I buy tastes the same. As do dozens of brands of U.S. beer.

There are 1,000 varieties of baseball cap, but it's almost impossible to buy any other kind of hat. There are ethnic restaurants with cuisines from all over the world, yet much of the food tastes strangely American.

The never-ending array of choices leads to less choice in other ways. The need for every store to offer a huge selection of products has virtually wiped out the small shopowner. There are no corner delis, no fruit stores, no small groceries in most neighborhoods — only chains like 7-Eleven.

Many items can be bought only in huge faceless malls that occupy every second city corner, with giant stores called Food City, Stereo City and Hardware City.

Every mall has the same stores, with the same design and the same products, from one corner of the country to the other. So every American city is starting to look the same — from L.A. to Miami.

It is survival of the biggest and blandest.

L.A. has 9 million people, but only one real daily newspaper — the L.A. Times — where opinions range from barely left of centre to fairly right. Londoners can choose from at least seven daily newspapers, while bilingual Montrealers have a choice of four. Even Ottawa has three.

The same lack of choice is seen in U.S. politics. Americans can choose from 70 types of steak sauce but only two political parties, and neither is as radical as Canada's Liberals, let alone the New Democratic Party.

Americans are sometimes more passionate about the symbols of freedom than the substance beneath them — from the Statue of Liberty to the right to bear arms. They have so much freedom to own handguns, they have lost the freedom to walk their streets. So much protection from "socialist-style Canadian medical care" that many have no care at all.

Since arriving here, I have seen a barrage of newspaper and TV stories attacking Bill Clinton's medicare plan. They say it would limit Americans' freedom to choose their doctor, choose their health plan, choose the date and hour of their open-heart surgery.

Yet a third of Americans can't afford any health coverage, and another third worry about losing it. I know middle-class Americans who won't let their kids go Rollerblading , because a small accident could bankrupt them. I know others who've stayed at jobs they hate for years, worried they will lose their health plan if they change companies.

In the pursuit of limitless freedom of choice, Americans give up some freedoms that people in countries like Canada enjoy. Even though our choice of jalapeño hamburger dressings is very limited.

Nervous Service

LOS ANGELES—I was in line for the cash at a large Montreal department store a few months ago when it became evident something was missing.

The cashier.

He was doing something more important than serving customers: he was taking inventory of every last product in his department. But no one complained. We were all veteran Canadian shoppers, long trained in the art of ignoring the fact you are being ignored.

Wander into a large department store in Montreal and you have to do a moose call to attract help. Even when you find it, you feel like you're asking for spare change.

It's not like that here in Los Angeles. Walk into an L.A. store and salespeople leap on you like cops on a mugger. Waiters fill your water glass five times and hand you the bill — before you've ordered a meal. Salespeople with name tags trail you around like bloodhounds, saying:

"Hi! I'm Greg. I'm a Capricorn. How may I help you today?"

Coffee-shop waitresses refill your coffee before you've ordered it. Ask them for a Coke and they say:

"Yes, sir! Would you like a Triple-Whopper, a fries and a supershake with that?"

At the city's busiest electronics shop, I was greeted by a fast-talking woman determined to sell me at least one thing I didn't need.

"How about a nice auto-focus underwater camera? A special on a self-programming recyclable VCR? A microwave popcorn-maker?

"You know, sir, that's a very nice shirt you have there. I think we have a matching stereo on the third floor."

And American sales staff don't even care if you buy anything.

"No trouble at all, sir. It was a pleasure showing you every item in the store. Please come back and *not* shop with us again."

In a recent poll of Canadians shopping in the U.S., half said they were there because the service was faster and friendlier than at home. Over-all, they said, salespeople in Canada were "sullen, silent and sluggish."

Why do Americans sales clerks hustle when ours hide? Why do they smile when we scowl? Are they happier people, cheerful to be paid three dollars an hour? Or do they smile in case the customer is carrying a gun? Maybe Canadians just don't know what official language to speak — making us terrified to try either.

Frankly, I don't know what causes Canadians to be service-stunted. But it's something deep in our collective psyche, as much a part of our national heritage as mosquitoes and medicare. And it's probably just as well.

America's frenzied friendliness doesn't end with your purchase. Once your "shopping experience" is over, you must tell them how you liked it by filling out cheerful Multiple-Choice Customer Questionnaires that now await you at every door:

Was your "super-service" super? Or just pretty friendly?

Was your taco burger good? Great? Or awesome?

How were the napkins? The toothpicks? The ice cubes? The linoleum?

Last spring I visited the Grand Canyon, where they ran mule rides down to the base of the canyon. At the end of my stay, my four-page "room-rating form" included questions asking me to:

"Rate your chambermaid. Rate your waitress. Rate your room service." There was even a question asking me (I am not making this up):

"Please rate your mule."

"Friendly," I wrote in the comments box. "But a little stubborn."

Frankly, when it comes to U.S. vs. Canadian-style service, I am torn. Much as I hate being ignored by salespeople, I hate it even more when they pay attention to me. I don't like clerks who follow me about, staring at me while I try to peek at the price tags.

I don't want to be on a first-name basis with my shoe salesman as he tells me about his rock-climbing trip up Mount Washington. I don't want to evaluate him in an exam after he leaves.

I want to shop — not have a relationship. For all my complaints, I guess I am as Canadian as those who serve me: as reclusive as they are elusive. At heart, I am a silent, sluggish, sullen shopper who secretly prefers to be ignored.

PLEASE RESPOND:

Did you like Mr. Freed's story?

Is it friendly enough? Funny enough? Too funny?

Should we give him a raise? Or give him the boot?

Please rate your mule.

Say Hi or Die

LOS ANGELES—I awoke at 2 a.m. yesterday in truly L.A. style, with a helicopter circling my street and a spotlight scouring the bushes. A megaphone voice was shouting:

"Don't move! We know you're there. Don't move!"

So I went back to sleep. I'm getting used to life in L.A. Lawless — the Dodge City of the '90s. As I write, I can hear the ever-present wail of sirens racing off toward muggings, murder and mayhem. The sky here is always sunny but to enjoy the weather it's wise to stay off the streets.

There were 1,100 homicides last year in L.A. proper— a city of 3.5 million people. Multiple murders that would be screaming headlines in Canada are buried on Page B6.

In the last month, a fired employee slaughtered three co-workers, a berserk professor shot his whole family, and a judge's son gunned own two policeman. A teenager put on Jim Morrison's song, "The End," and killed his father with an AR-15 assault rifle. Then he killed a policewoman, and himself.

The L.A. police union has just launched a pressure campaign, sending out letters to travel agents and tour groups. "Do not come to Los Angeles ... it is not safe," they warn tourists, though L.A. citizens have known that for years.

The city is an armed and alarmed camp.

"Car jackings! Muggings! Thieves! These are the facts of L.A. life!" screamed a full-page newspaper ad this week for a sale on car alarms, with features like an "emergency panic button."

I wandered into a shop called Gun Heaven (telephone: 938-GUNS) and there weren't many hunting rifles to be seen, only weapons for hunting people. The shelves were stocked with handguns, "hellfire triggers" and "hide-a-holsters." The walls were covered in T-shirts that showed a smoking gun and the words:

"I DON'T dial 911."

"How do I get a gun?" I asked a short young man with a big gun on his hip, who said his name was V.J.

"Have you used one before?" he asked cheerily.

"No?, Well, that's no problem, as long as you've got a valid driver's license."

He handed me a small registration form, in triplicate, with some boxes to check off attesting I wasn't a felon, drug addict or psychotic mass murderer. And if I was, would I tell him?

Then he showed me a choice of gleaming handguns from the *Bounty Hunter* at $350, to a "$99.99 special" that sounded like a disposable coffee filter.

"You use it once then throw it away," said V.J.

For home protection, V.J. advised a 12-gauge shotgun. "A revolver is easier to get at, but a 12-gauge scares guys off faster, especially when you pump a couple of rounds into the rack.

"It packs a lot of visual impact."

When I said I was from Canada, V.J. was more impressed than if I'd pulled out an Uzi. "You moved from Montreal to L.A.!? Man, you're crazy! That's like going from heaven to hell."

He's right. American cities like L.A. have become eerie combat zones, where you are always instinctively on guard. Like most people here I now think twice before parking on a side street.

I gauge how far I must walk, how many doorwells I must pass, and what kind of people. I never walk outside at night, and why would I want to? The only people on the streets carry bedrolls.

Restaurants and bars usually provide someone to take the risk of parking your car. It's called "valet parking" — a polite way of saying: PARKING YOURSELF MAY REDUCE LIFE EXPECTANCY.

After a while you don't even think about walking any more. You forget you ever did, along with other simple pleasures we take for granted in Canada. You don't go to see interesting sights like the Watts tower, because it is in Watts. You don't look at other drivers, because they may be looking at you.

You become suspicious of the homeless, of panhandlers, of anyone who looks weird, or different than you. And you understand why many Americans are now obsessed with Law and Order, instead of justice.

California has recently passed a tough "three strikes and you're out" law, that will automatically throw people in jail for 25 years after their third felony, even if they've only stolen an orange.

Many police and politicians here admit the new law is unfair and may double the number of jails. But Californians strongly support it and other states are soon expected to follow. It's a snappy solution with a snappy American name; if baseball only had two strikes, the law might be worse.

Americans want revenge and it's easier to throw people in jail after they shoot you than to figure out ways to stop them from shooting you; easier to arm the entire country than to disarm it.

After all, a city full of guns does have some advantages. Motorists in L.A. are more polite than those back home in Montreal, partly because they are terrified of offending other drivers.

"Don't honk," said a friend to me recently, when a car swerved in front of us. "They may be armed!"

I suspect guns also contribute to the city's fervor for friendliness, which I've mentioned in other stories. In a land where anyone may have a gun, you chat with strangers partly to be friendly, but partly to make sure they are "normal" like you.

Like other big American cities, L.A.'s friendliness has a slightly defensive edge. The city's motto could be: "Say hi or die."

Gavel-gazing

LOS ANGELES—I was at a dinner party recently with a crowd of screenwriters, producers and other Hollywood types when all eyes turned to the door for the arrival of a hot new celebrity.

No, it wasn't Julia Roberts or Jay Leno. It was a witness in the trial of the Menendez brothers — two Beverly Hills kids accused of murdering their parents, in the recent mega-trial to sweep this town.

The rest of the night, the "witness" held court with gossipy stories about the Menendezes — a kind of *All in the Dysfunctional Family*, in which Meathead actually shoots Archie.

Everyone at the party had seen the "witness" testify on live TV and thought he was great, "very credible . . . very natural," perfect for a role as a juror in the Menendez movie. It all sounded a lot like show business, because it is.

Canadian courts are still a shadowy world where the only glimpse of the action is an artist's sketch. Judges are quick to ban publication of details in some cases, as in the Karla Homolka case where some testimony has been sealed "in perpetuity."

But here in the land of made-for-TV liberty, justice has become so transparent it's practically embarrassing. From Rodney King and the Denny case to Nancy Kerrigan and the Battling Bobbitts, there's a new star under the lights every week.

Court figures are becoming cult figures.

The liveliest action takes place on Court TV, a channel dedicated entirely to televised court cases. The schedule features a surreal parade of pedophiles, penis-severers, parent-killers, baby-smotherers, freeway-shooters, arsonists, muggers, molesters and other accused criminals telling their story to the judge and a huge TV audience.

This week's hottest shows included:

●*Prime Time Justice*, featuring the "live plea-bargain" by skater Tonya Harding's ex-husband.

●*Lock and Key*, starring ex-Charles Manson cult member Patricia

Krenwinkel begging for release at a live parole hearing.

●*Instant Justice*, with live weeping testimony from a mother accused of killing her baby and burying it in the front yard.

During slow moments of testimony, Don Cherry-style legal experts give colorful play-by-play commentary:

Expert: Ohhh, that was a beautiful cross-examination by the prosecution! She set the witness up with some lob-balls, then caught her with a savage question that caught the defence lawyer napping.

I'd say it was a triple play, maybe even a home run, and a likely trial winner!

Anchor: Thanks for your thoughts, Judge Thompson. Now stay tuned — coming up after this break — highlights from the sentencing! Then, the strange case of a three-year-old who shot her mother on "orders from God."

People in L.A. can't step outside their doors without worrying they will be gunned down in a drive-by shooting. But at least they can stay home and enjoy watching the criminals face the music.

Personally, I find watching Court TV creepy, tawdry and strangely addictive. I feel like a guilty Peeping Tom, unable to stop myself from looking into someone else's window.

I am intrigued by Lyle Menendez's toupée and his brother's $250,000 credit-card spending limit. I know more about John Bobbitt's penis than my own.

I know more details of the Homolka case than I did when I was in Canada, because they've been published in most U.S. papers. But I don't know if any of it makes for more justice, or just more entertainment.

Canadian courts could use less press censorship, but like everything in the U.S. there's a short distance between liberty and lunacy. The Menendez jurors had barely pronounced their verdict when they were mobbed by TV crews offering cash-filled envelopes in exchange for their story.

Two TV films on the Menendez trial are now under way, and will be finished before the case has been retried. Will a made-for-TV jury decide the case before the real one does?

The Kerrigan-Harding story had barely started before scores of film producers were fighting over the TV and movie rights.

What next? Will Mafia hitmen start asking for a piece of the action, too?

-OK Bugsy, whaddya gonna charge to knock off two cops?

-Geez, Frankie, cops are risky. I want $15,000 a hit and 5 points of gross receipts on any made-for-TV movies.

As the line between justice and entertainment blurs, viewers here might not settle for just watching trials. They'll want to take part in the judgment, too.

A jury of 30 million truly ordinary citizens will follow the whole case from their living rooms. Then they'll dial 1-800-UB-DA-JUDGE and pronounce their verdict by pressing:

1. For acquittal
2. For manslaughter
3. To execute

If more than two-thirds of the audience presses 3, the defendant will be electrocuted immediately. Instant U.S.-style "takeout" justice — no muss, no fuss, no appeals.

What about the rights of the criminals? I guess they can always publish books.

Posthumously.

Hapless Holiday

LOS ANGELES—Happy Holiday to me, if not to you.

Here in the U.S., February 21 is Presidents' Day: an important American national day, as you can tell from big newspaper ads promoting patriotic events like the Presidents' Day Linen Sale and the Presidents' Day Triple Bonus Mattress Event.

Technically, this holiday celebrates the fact we're halfway between Lincoln's and Washington's birthdays, but it's really just an excuse for Americans to take yet another winter break.

This is the second three-day weekend since I arrived in Los Angeles last month. Jan. 17 was Martin Luther King Day. Some states have also declared extra holidays, like Louisiana, which celebrated Battle of New Orleans Day and Robert E. Lee Day in January.

Talk about any excuse for a holiday.

During the same period, Canadians have been suffering through the Great Winter Holiday Famine — a grim annual stretch from January 1 to early April, without a single day off.

No wonder Easter feels like a miracle when it arrives.

I've never understood why Canada doesn't have a mid-winter break, exactly when we need one most. In nice weather, our governments find any pretext to give us time off.

We celebrate Queen Victoria's birthday in May, though Britain stopped marking the event a quarter-century ago. In Quebec, we celebrate St. Jean Baptiste Day on June 24, and Canada Day a week later. Then we take construction holidays, school holidays and summer vacations.

Frankly, by the time Labor Day arrives, I am ready for a Work Day.

Not that I'm knocking holidays. But why not save one for mid-winter, when just being alive is reason to celebrate?

Must we be a nation of masochists, denying ourselves any chance of pleasure during winter? Or are our politicians so depressed in winter they can't find the energy to declare a holiday?

If the U.S. can find two reasons for mid-winter breaks, why can't we? Some people say it's expected of us under NAFTA's rules on fair competition.

But what holidays should we mark? Combing through Canadian

historical dates, I can't find any prime ministers or very famous Canadians born in February (though lots of them seem to die that month).

In fact, nothing good ever seems to happen in mid-winter.

Ships get launched in May, while cornerstones are laid in June. Rebellions are fought in the spring, when the snow melts, and treaties are signed in the fall before it starts snowing again.

Both Canada and the U.S. were born in July, probably so the founding fathers wouldn't get stuck in a snowstorm and miss the signings.

The only memorable events that happen during Canadian winters are disasters: fires, storms, gas explosions, power blackouts. Look back at Canada's winters and you'll find almost every major disaster in our country's history:

The Great Halifax Explosion (December 1917); the Springhill Mine Disaster (February 1891); the sinking of the Ocean Ranger (February 1984); the Hinton Train Disaster (February 1986); the introduction of the GST (January 1991).

People get cabin fever in February and do disastrous things. René Lévesque ran over a derelict. Claude Charron stole a sports jacket. The Conservatives elected Joe Clark as leader. Maybe we should take a hint and choose a winter holiday as grim as our life in winter. In fact, it would be very Canadian.

In her book *Survival*, Margaret Atwood found that characters in Canadian novels traditionally get killed by the environment — dying by frostbite, drowning, avalanche or forest fire.

Canadian movies, too, often feature great hardship and suffering, from gruelling winter epics like *Kamouraska* to gruelling summer epics like *Black Robe*.

We write books about the Halifax Explosion and songs about the sinking of the Edmund Fitzgerald on the Great Lakes. Why should our holidays be different?

It's time we had a national winter holiday that expressed our national winter mood. Let's mark a winter break by recalling a terrible January avalanche, a great February power blackout, or just a spectacularly awful winter day.

How about a holiday called Great Snowfall Day, to commemorate the 118 centimetres that fell at Lake Lakelse, B.C, on Jan. 17, 1974?

Or Great Frostbite Day, marking Feb. 3, 1947, when the temperature fell to minus-63 in Snag, Yukon?

It's time Canadians learned to celebrate our suffering properly. A miserable season deserves a miserable holiday, to properly express our nation's mood.

So, for now, have an unhappy Presidents' Day, and go to work. I'll be spending it patriotically — at the Special Presidents' Day, Post-Earthquake Fire Sale Tire Sale.

As the Olympic Word Turns

LOS ANGELES—Help!

I am a captive of U.S. Olympics coverage. I am trapped in Tonya and Nancy's Norwegian Adventure. My only sources of Olympic information are Greg Gumbel and David Letterman's mom.

I know why Americans flunk geography. If you watched the Olympics on American TV, you'd think there were only five countries in the world: America and the four countries they have to beat to win a gold medal.

Friends at home tell me Canada is having its best year in Olympic history— but watching the coverage here, I didn't even know we were competing. Throughout my life I have watched the Olympics on Canadian TV and foolishly believed they were about sports and international competition: the fastest skaters, the most daring skiers, the silliest looking luge racers.

But here in the U.S., the Olympics aren't a world sports event at all — they are a huge national soap opera starring heroic Americans who struggle to overcome adversity.

As the Olympic World Turns.

Every event features an American Olympic "hero" grasping for gold — after overcoming disease, poverty, and crooked teeth. Half the first week's coverage in Los Angeles involved Tonya Harding, whose tough-luck story bumped Bosnia out of the headlines.

I watched a "live exclusive news report" of Tonya's truck getting a parking ticket, saw her eat Slurpies at a 7-Eleven shop on a hidden TV camera, then catch a bouquet of flowers in a dozen slow-motion replays.

But now Tonya's 15,000 minutes of fame are over. She has disappeared, replaced by new athletes who have overcome injury, illness and no endorsements to make America proud. Typical coverage sounds like this:

"And there go the skaters in this 1,000-metre event!! — with U.S. skater Debbie, the Dallas dynamo, in last place! But it's truly a triumph that Debbie has even come this far."

CUT to childhood photos of Debbie and start violin music.

"Debbie's dad was killed in a bank holdup the day Debbie competed in her first big race. Debbie's mom worked cleaning dog kennels to help

Debbie get here."

CUT to tearful interviews with Debbie's chiropractor, sports therapist, bungee-jumping instructor, psychic channeler and dental hygienist.

RETURN to announcer: "And now let's go back to the rink where the race has ended. Apparently some Norwegian guy has just set a new world record — but Debbie finished a strong 19th.

"We've got five reporters waiting to get her reaction."

Why doesn't Canada glorify its heroes like this? Why don't we turn our athletes into national soap-opera heroes? Why isn't Myriam Bédard known as Annie Oakley on Skis, or The Queen of Run-and-Gun. Why isn't Elvis Stojko the King of Rock and Triple-toe Roll?

Are we too private, too self-deprecating a nation to engage in this kind of hype? Or could it be that our athletes wouldn't know what to say — they'd be too embarrassed.

America loves to celebrate the individual, the rags-to-riches urchin who conquers adversity to get a $1-million movie deal and a contract for Jello endorsements. Ordinary heroes dominate their soap operas, talk shows and day-to-day life. Here in Los Angeles, everyone has their own heroic life story that they are always ready to tell you at the drop of a hat.

In the last week alone, my Mexican car mechanic told me how he climbed fences and swam rivers to get to the U.S., and give his son the American Dream. My cab driver told me how he went from riches to rags to driving a cab. And my barber told me how he survived war in Ukraine, famine in Poland and poverty on New York's east side to get where he is today.

"I'm a miracle, a living miracle. They could write a book about me — no, two books. Are you interested?"

You'd have to know a Canadian for a lifetime before he'd tell you these stories, but in the U.S. it's just a way of opening a conversation.

This is reflected in the Olympics. Ask an American athlete why she won a bronze medal and she'll give you a tearful, heroic story that's the basis of a blockbuster film script.

Ask a Canadian gold-medal winner how she did it and she'll say:

"It was nothing. I just hung in and got lucky. Anyone could have done it."

Maybe, but only a Canadian would say so.

The World's Best Column

LOS ANGELES—Venice Beach is a circus without a tent, an oceanside boardwalk filled with kooks, quacks and California characters.

There are Romanian crystal-ball gazers and Cherokee Indian past-life readers; musclebound outdoor weightlifters and vegetarians with signs saying "Meat is Murder!" There are young people out to "Legalize Marijuana" and a 70-year-old woman wearing Rollerblades who calls herself Skateboard Granny.

Venice has been called the place where the flakes settle when you tilt the American continent. Yet even here, on the fringes of America, you know this is a land of hustle and hype.

"The World's Best Massage!" says a sign at a makeshift massage stall. "Melt into your chair with the Muscle-melter. Then try the Jell-O-maker!"

A nearby sausage stand promises the "World's Best Hot Dog" while a competitor shouts: "Tempt your tummy with the best pizza on the planet!"

Even a weathered old homeless man asleep on the sidewalk has a sign saying: "World's Best Wino. I sing, I dance. I tell stories."

And he does, if you wake him up.

As I arrive at the end of my stay in L.A., there are many things I won't miss: the crime, the homelessness, the racial division. But I'd love to bottle America's entrepreneurial energy and take it back to my home and complacent land.

When Canadians think something is good, we say it's "not bad," trying not to toot our own horn. When Americans think something is good, they say it's "Great! Fabulous! Unbelievable!"

Canadian salespeople practically hide behind the counter until customers ask for help. Talented Canadians quietly wait to be discovered.

But Americans rarely wait for opportunity to knock at the door. They pound the door down. Phone numbers here are seen as a free chance to advertise your business: 1-800 YOU-DENT. 1-800 FIX-FEET. 1-800-GET-MACE.

Public services have catchy names you won't forget, like MOTOR-

VOTER and LOAN-BY-PHONE. Every car license plate is a poor man's billboard: I 2N PIANO. Or I SUE EM. Or just a smarmy U2NVME, on a Jag.

Even ordinary Americans are quick to promote themselves, pitching their virtues as soon as they meet you:

"Hi! I'm David and I write screenplays, do carpentry and wash windows. Here's my card." In Canada, we wait politely until someone asks us what we do.

Canadians think it's in bad taste to promote yourself, but Americans think it's in bad taste if you don't.

"What's the matter? Are you too arrogant to sell yourself like everyone else?"

People here are always searching for a fresh angle. A taco chain promises "60-Second Drive-Thru Service, or You Eat Free!" A truck-stop in the Midwest has highway billboards saying: "Free 72-ounce steak!— IF you eat it in under an hour!"

Competition is the lifeblood of American society, partly because there's no safety net if you lose. The winners win and the losers lose. The cost of this is a lot of hardship and homelessness, but there is an up side.

It forces people to use their wits, and many find ingenious ways to make a living.

There is a self-appointed "doorman" at our post office who offers better advice than the postal clerk. "Try the certified mail, sir, it's cheaper than a registered letter and just as fast… Now, can you spare a quarter? I'm homeless and this is how I make my living."

We have met freelance "information guides" in the San Francisco subway and freelance "traffic attendants" in crowded theatre parking lots who help you find a spot.

One man put a quarter into an outdoor parking meter and locked it into the "paid" position with a paper clip. "You just park as long as you want, ma'am," he said gently, "though I'd appreciate any contribution you can make."

Even panhandlers have a clever pitch. One, near our house, carries a cardboard sign that reads: "I take Visa and MasterCard."

Half of every American transaction is the spiel that comes with it, the sizzle on the steak. Everything is always "ON SALE!" at "SENSATIONAL PRICES!"

Nothing is sold at "retail prices" and nothing comes in "small" containers

— what kind of advertising is that? Everything comes in medium, large, extra-large and humungous. Even second-hand furniture is advertised as "Fabulous Pre-owned Furnishings!"

Canada's reluctance to promote our products, ourselves, or our country is our national neurosis — our insecurity blanket. Americans celebrate whatever they do, while Canadians tend to put ourselves down, even when we do things well.

After living in the U.S. for almost five months, I think America's violence makes Quebec sovereignty look like a minor problem. And America's social problems make our country seem like a charmed land.

Yet despite their problems, Americans still believe they live in the "greatest country on earth," and Canadians are always complaining our country doesn't work.

As somebody once said: "Canada's national bird is the grouse."

Frankly, after six months in Los Angeles, I think there's nothing wrong with Canada a little U.S.- style marketing couldn't cure. An American ad agency could do wonders for our image.

It would say Canada is the kindest, gentlest country on earth. It would say we have the biggest mountains, the best hockey players, the coldest weather and the warmest hearts.

It would say Canada is "America with a heart."

And for a change it wouldn't even be exaggerating.

CHAPTER SIX

Anarchy and Bureaucracy
(+ GST)

H.R. Freed

NOWADAYS, when people ask my profession, I no longer say: "writer." I say "tax collector," because that's how I spend most of my life — like a growing number of Canadians.

Instead of sitting at my word processor crafting sentences, I hunch over my calculator, figuring out my "QST exigible" and my "Input Tax Adjustment." I craft invoices. I calculate other people's taxes. I phone and harass them to pay. I file 16 tax reports a year.

Like the Kafka character who wakes up to find he is a cockroach, I have suddenly been transformed into something grotesque:

I am a taxman for the federal and provincial government. Here is my story:

My transmogrification began in 1991, when the Canadian government introduced the GST. Like everyone, I hated paying it, but soon I discovered far worse:

Under the new tax law, self-employed writers like me were considered a "service." Everytime I wrote anything, I had to charge my "employers" GST of 7%, collect it, and send it to Ottawa with a detailed tax report.

I had become a tax accountant: H.R. Freed.

It was awful, but I gave it a shot, sending out GST invoices along with every $50 newspaper story I wrote. Unfortunately, many of my "employers" hated the GST and refused to send it to me, so I had to call and hound them in my new capacity as tax inspector.

"Hello," I found myself saying to magazine editors and TV producers. "I notice you didn't include your tax payment along with my cheque. I'm afraid I have to insist that you pay your taxes *immediately!*"

Some argued, others cursed me. One editor insisted her magazine was a cultural institution that would be destroyed by paying GST. A TV producer argued his station was a public institution and should be exempt. A left-wing magazine accused me of being a "mole" for Revenue Canada.

They refused to pay.

Meanwhile, I got threatening letters from the federal government demanding I forward the taxes these people owe or *I* would be charged with tax evasion.

Things came to a crisis last year with the introduction of the Quebec Provincial Sales Tax (PST). Now I am a provincial "service" too, forced to bill 6.5% provincial tax on top of my 7 % federal one. I must file 12 PST reports a year along with my 4 GST reports — 16 tax reports a year — which doesn't leave me a lot of time to write.

I used to dream of writing the great Canadian novel. Now the best I can hope for is the great Canadian tax form.

A few weeks ago, I received something called a monthly PST "Work Chart," I am expected to fill out every month for the rest of my life. Let me share some of the early paragraphs, verbatim:

Total supplies. Enter total value exluding GST and QST of the taxable, non-taxable, tax-exempt and zero-rated property and services you provided. Do not include immovables. Carry this amount to box 201.

Total of QST eligible and adjustments. Add boxes A, B and C and carry the result to box 203.

Total of Input Tax Refund (ITRs) and adjustments.

If you don't understand this, neither do several hundred thousand other self-employed Canadians who are supposed to fill it out. I know writers, artists, actors, clowns, carpenters and cabbies, all as bewildered by their new tax-collecting job as me.

Recently I ran into a lawyer friend who had spent three days trying to catch up on a year's backlog of GST and PST. He wasn't sure whether to change professions or change countries.

I've spent sleepless nights trying to figure out what I've collected and what I haven't, what I owe and what others owe. But the figures never seem to add up correctly, so I'm scared to send them in.

I feel like a tax evader, and I'm not even evading my own taxes. I don't mind paying taxes, but I do mind working for the tax department, and frankly, I am not cut out for the job. I became a writer partly because I can't stand paperwork, bureaucracy or numbers. I can barely figure out my phone bill.

Why must I do volunteer work for the tax departments?

I am ready to serve my country in other capacities. I could write PR for the Prime Minister. I could spy for the RCMP at press conferences. Anything but this.

In Kafka's story, the character never escapes his new identity and ultimately faces a cockroach's death, crushed under the mindless heel of the modern world. I keep hoping I will soon wake up and discover I am a writer again, before the same thing happens to me.

Read at Your Own Risk

WARNING:

The following story contains flammable paper, smudgy ink and words that may cause drowsiness. Those reading it do so with the knowledge that sarcasm, irony, hyperbole and other cheap literary devices may be employed. The reader accepts these risks and the danger of irritation and offence thereto.

If blurred vision, heavy eyelids, headaches or nausea occur, STOP READING IMMEDIATELY and consult physician. These may be symptoms of overdose.

Pretty much everything you pick up these days comes with some kind of warning, from kitchenware to teddy bears. The warnings preceding TV programs are usually more interesting than the programs themselves: "The following scenes may contain disturbing images, graphic language, nude bodies and lust-crazed sex."

And this is before a car commercial.

The warning labels on cigarette packs, like SMOKING REDUCES LIFE EXPECTANCY and SMOKING IS A MAJOR CAUSE OF CANCER are so large you'd think that's why people bought them. Now, the federal government says it wants to make these warnings bigger. If so, they'll have to enlarge the package.

Many warnings assume that human beings are at the same level on the evolutionary scale as a Cocker Spaniel. Take the bathroom, a place filled with life-threatening items like:

- DANGER! Shaver: Do not use in shower!
- CAUTION! Hair Dryer: Do not use while asleep!
- BEWARE! Shower: May contain very hot water!

The warnings in my medicine cabinet could scare off Timothy Leary. Take something for a headache and the possible side-effects may include nausea, heartburn, dizziness, rapid eye movement, scurvy, bubonic fever and black plague.

Suddenly, a headache sounds fine.

If you're pregnant or nursing, don't bother to open the medicine chest.

You can't swallow anything but water, and it's wise to consult a doctor first.

Not that I'm against health warnings, but I sometimes wonder who they're trying to protect — the consumer or the company. I was cross-country skiing in Vermont recently and my trail ticket had more fine print than a mortgage contract. I quote:

> "The purchaser of this ticket purchases and uses it with the understanding that skiing is a hazardous sport; that bare spots, ice, changing snow, bumps, stumps, stones, trees and other hazards and obstructions exist in any ski area.
>
> "The purchaser realizes that falls and collisions are common and numerous and that injuries can result ... and he accepts the hazards of the sport and the danger of injury incident thereto."

Before I stepped into my skis, I called my lawyer. Warning fever rises sharply when you cross into the U.S., along with the number of lawyers. Even the most innocuous items have warnings.

My neighbor's made-in-the-U.S. frisbee actually comes with this important note of caution:

"DO NOT USE EXCEPT IN CLEAR SPACE WITH AN ALERT CATCHER."

As opposed to what? Throwing it at someone who's asleep at the dinner table?

The warning epidemic would have pleased my Aunt Ida, a worry-wart who haunted my childhood. Ida was convinced everything on Earth was dangerous: knives, forks, spoons — and especially anything with wires.

"Don't touch that lamp!" she'd yell, as you went to plug it in. "You'll get electrocuted!"

"Don't touch that TV antenna! It'll blow up!"

When Ida's son went off to college in another city she gave him a warning, too. "Don't speak to strangers," she said, even though he didn't know anyone else.

Back then, I thought Ida was paranoid. Today I realize she was just ahead of her time. Ida knew that the only way to protect yourself from life is to avoid it — eat nothing, touch nothing, speak to no one.

She knew the world is a dangerous place, and that being alive is a serious risk to your health. She'd have made a great lawyer. In fact, in a few years, I suspect everything will have Aunt Ida-like warnings, such as:

CAUTION

EGG. Cook before eating.
Do not swallow whole.
Contains cholesterol and sharp bits of shell.
Expiry date: 3 weeks

Until then, however, I suggest you simply:

Quit Worrying About Your Health.
It Will Go Away.

Secretly Me

"VISA SERVICE CENTRE" said the telephone tape recording. "All our operators are busy. Please stay on the line to retain your calling priority."

Grrrrr.

I was in on-hold hell and getting madder by the minute. I fumed. I plotted. I could feel the secret me escaping from its cage. I had called Visa to complain about the interest it had charged me for paying late. It was the standard 2500 % a day all credit companies charge — but this time I was pretty convinced I had mailed my cheque on time.

Grrrrrrrrrrrr.

As I waited the secret me took over, preparing my response. Visa would regret the day it messed with me. I would cancel my Visa card and take out a Master Card instead -— as well as an American Express card, a Petrocan card and a Provigo card. Any card but theirs.

I would get a Schwartz's Deli silver card. A Dilallo-Burger gold card. A Bagel Factory platinum-plus-cream-cheese-and-lox card. They would *pay.*

I would write a letter to the government demanding an investigation into interest rates. I would go on a door-to-door campaign across the nation urging people to cancel their Visa cards. I would single-handedly *bring down* VISA.

"Visa Service Centre," said a gentle voice on the other end of the phone, interupting my internal tirade. "Norma speaking. How may I help you?"

"Oh ... uh ... hi," I said, and suddenly the secret me was fading, replaced by another character: quiet, complacent, Walter Mittyish me.

"I was wondering if you could help me," I said politely. "I just got my monthly statement, and well ... I was hoping you could take a look at it ... just to, uh, double check a figure ... if you don't mind."

Sighhh.

It seems I am doomed to live a double life: one, my dull and obsequious real life and the other a bold fantasy life that goes on inside my head. My real life is spent doing tedious, annoying, humiliating things. I stand silently in line at banks and supermarkets. I sit drumming my fingers on hold on the phone. I peer down Metro tunnels waiting for the train. I stew in traffic, silently cursing other drivers, who are probably cursing me. I am ignored by busy waitresses, abused by indifferent clerks, and snubbed by civil servants — as I wait politely, rarely losing my cool.

But things are different in my secret life. There, I am a brash, belligerent even bullying creature who takes no guff from anyone. I lecture lead-footed postal clerks about their "fat swivel service jobs." I leave notes for nasty waitresses saying: "Since you ignored my table, I'm ignoring your tip."

I stop obnoxious speeding drivers and say: "Citizen's arrest, buddy! That'll cost you a $7000 ticket!"

All without ever saying a word in my real life.

When I am stuck five minutes in a bank line-up my secret life shouts to the crowd: "It's OUR money!— let's take it back!" — and leads an attack on the bank manager's office. Meanwhile, my real self inches up in line.

I brilliantly contest parking tickets and property tax bills. I launch court cases against hotels who charge me $4.50 per phone call — and I win millions.

In my secret life I always win, no matter how big my adversary. I have privatized the post office, I have bankrupted major corporations, I have brought down governments, fired prime ministers and forced high-flying mayors to work at minimum wage.

I am a terror in my imagination but a wimp in real life.

Why can't I live up to my secret life? Why don't I vent my feelings, express my anger, bring my fantasies to life? Partly because I know that half the people I am fantasizing about are having similar fantasies about me.

The waitress I am secretly lecturing for slow service is also silently lecturing me: "Why couldn't you order your Coke before I finished adding up your bill, jerk? And who cares if you like your eggs 'crisp on the outside, but medium squishy inside?'"

The truck driver who has infuriated me by roaring past on the inside lane of the highway is thinking: "What are you driving in the fast lane for, buddy, if you're gonna slow down to sightsee every time you pass a grazing cow?"

The Visa lady listening to me explain how I mailed my bill on time is thinking: "Gimme a break, mister. I've heard better excuses from my five-year-old child."

If we all let our secret lives out of the closet at the same time the real world would be a pretty noisy and intolerable place. No, it's better to be a wimp, I figure — living out in my mind what I will never do in life. And sometimes getting surprised by the results.

Take the Visa operator. She listened politely to my excuse, checked my bill and offerred to cancel my interest charge — although now that I've calmed down and thought about it, I'm not even sure I was right.

So for the time being the secret me has relented and decided not to bankrupt Visa. Besides it is too busy making more important plans. It seems we're taking Hydro-Québec and cable TV to the Supreme Court over this morning's bills.

Voice Jail

WELCOME TO . . . JOSH FREED's . . . AUTOMATED COLUMN!
Our writer is currently occupied. Please stay on the page to retain your reading priority. If you know the kind of column you desire, you can save time by making the following selection.
—To read about pigeons, PRESS 1 and turn to page 35.
— For a Dave Barry column, PRESS 2 and buy another collection of columns.
— If you'll read anything, PRESS ON.
Beep.

Sorry, just trying to keep up with the times. Like many people, I spend much of my life in telephone limbo these days, being shuttled around from call-forwarding to call-waiting, call-answering, call-screening and call-demeaning.

Government offices have all switched over to the new "interactive" phone systems and soon we will be banking, shopping, dating and mating this way. The euphemism is "voice mail" — but it should be called voice jail, because it's almost impossible to escape.

Typically, it goes something like this:

Beep. Hello. Thanks for calling "No-People Airlines." All our operators have been fired. Please stay on the line and prepare to be humiliated by computer.

Beep. For flight information about northeastern routes, Tuesday and Saturday, May 13 through July 7, PRESS 1.
— For advance booking for three or more people, weekdays, from noon to 4 p.m. and 6 to 9 a.m., excluding Wednesdays, PRESS 2.
— To speak to an agent, prepare three days of food and water by your phone, and PRESS 3.

Some airlines take a more intimate approach, and allow you to answer the computer's questions orally instead of pushing buttons.

i.e.:

If you require flight information, please say YES immediately after the tone. Otherwise...REMAIN SILENT. *Beep.*

Correctly answer a skill-testing question and more complicated questions will follow. Would you like current flight information or future Tourgroup information?

Do you wish to change your reservation, and if so, what is your flight number? Your mother's maiden name? Your bank balance?

Try phoning the Canadian citizenship office and you'll spend 30 minutes pressing buttons, answering questions like:

"Are you a foreign-born national with Canadian-born parents? Or a Canadian-born nationalist with foreign-born children? Do you have a registered driver's licence and Medicare card? A Social Insurance number and Canadian Tire card?

"What is your weight in centimetres? Can you convert this to Farenheit?"

Frankly, anyone who can answer all the questions should be made a citizen immediately. The computer should ask you to name the nation's capital and the Prime Minister — then swear you in and sing "O Canada."

The worst thing about the new voice jailers is their attitude. Old-time secretaries had unpredicatable, colorful personalities, with raspy voices, crotchety tempers and strange accents. Even the old answering machines had entertaining messages like:

"Hi! This is Ralph! Wait till the beep — it's coming soon — any minute now...I think?

"Hmmm...Honey! How do you make this thing wo–"

"*Beep.*"

The new voice-mail systems are answered by cool, patronizing voices that treat you like a psychiatrist trying to calm down a lunatic waving a gun. They speak slowly, as if talking to a ten-year old — but even this is hard to focus on long before your mind drifts and you miss a question.

So some companies are now introducing super-slow messages that treat you as if you were 4.

"I – am – sorry. You – failed – to – push – the – right– buttons. You – are – not – smart – enough – for – our – regular – phone – system.

"Please — Push — 1 — to — use — our — remedial — system.

"*Beep.*"

"Push — 1 — now — blockhead."

Thanks for reading Mr. Freed's column. If you'd like to read it again, REMAIN SILENT. If you'd like to read something funnier, try Doonesbury.

This column is now out of service. Please turn the page now. Turn the page NOW . . .

Don't Mess With My Mess

I'VE RECENTLY BEEN TAKING PART in a giant toxic-waste cleanup: the Exxon Valdez of Esplanade Avenue, the Chernobyl of the home-pollution world.

I am cleaning my desk.

Imagine a ceiling-high pyramid of paper: a leaning tower of yellowed newspapers, leaky pens, unpaid parking tickets, bailiff notices, old pizza boxes and petrified coffee cups. All that's missing is a sign that says: DANGER: LIFE-THREATENING MESS.

You might have seen a glimpse of it in a film I was in about anglo-Quebecers recently. People are always stopping to talk to me about it. Not the film — the mess.

"Is your office really like that?" they ask in amazement. "How can you find anything?"

Well, the truth is that my mess isn't just any mess. It's the best system of desk mess available — for a messy person like me. I have come to this conclusion after years of studying alternative styles of desk mess management.

Which are you?

●**Pseudo-neat Mess:** You stuff every scrap of paper you get into a desk drawer or filing cabinet, until it is crammed full, and never open it again. Your office always looks spotless, but if you accidentally open a cupboard you will be crushed under a 20-year collection of Consumers Distributing magazines and unopened electricity bills.

●**Mound manager:** You carefully divide the chaos into dozens of perfectly stacked piles that cover every centimetre of your desk and floor space.

"Watch that pile!" you shout, as visitors squeeze between two six-foot piles of files. "Those are my income-tax records for the 1970s!"

"And don't touch those shoeboxes! They've got my high-school compositions in them."

●**Developer:** You are the Donald Trump of the mess world. As soon as you mess one surface, you search for new spaces to fill — from the top of your microwave to the inside of your dishwasher. When you run out of surfaces, you build new shelves and extensions until there is no room left in your office for you — because even your chair is piled high with files.

As a developer you are easy to spot. When someone phones, you never answer until the sixth ring. You are tracking down the phone by its sound, because you have no idea what pile it is under.

●**Archeologist:** my own system. The older the paper, the deeper down in my mess it is, like the ruins of a Roman town built over a Greek temple. My 1991 tax returns are about six geological layers above the phone number of the window washer I used in 1985. I never know what I'll find on a dig.

Three days into my most recent excavation, I suddenly struck wood! It was my desk, which I hadn't seen in over a year.

Since then I've unearthed:

—My 1991 agenda (the final entry is dated Feb. 3, the last time I saw it).

— An undeveloped roll of film from a trip to the Soviet Union, when there still was one.

— A $15 gift certificate from Classic's bookstore.

The trouble with the archeological system is it's hard to know what to throw out. Who knows what objects history will prove valuable?

Should I throw out my 1981 driver's license? My ticket stub from last year's jazz festival?

How about the 1987 Montreal phone book? Yeah, I guess I could dump it, since I do have the entire collection from 1988 to 1994.

My desk disorder extends to my mobile home, my car, so cluttered with books, newspapers, scraps of paper, Styrofoam cups, skates and ski wax that passengers must carry whatever they displace, in their lap.

Several years ago, the car was badly vandalized when someone tried to rip the trunk off the hinges with a crowbar. A police officer peered into the car and said:

"My God! The filthy animals! What did they take?"

"Well," I mumbled, half under my breath, "they never actually got inside."

From the look on the officer's face, I thought she was going to charge *me* with vandalism.

Sometimes I weary of my mess, but still I prefer it to the empty desk of my opposite type — the obsessive desk organizer. This person has a desk so clean it gleams. The shelves are so neatly stacked with envelopes and color-coded files, you'd think he or she ran a stationery store.

I get nervous around desks like these. I suspect their owners do nothing all day but clean and file things and never have time to use them.

In fact, a recent study in Germany found people with messy desks actually find things faster than people with neat desks. I was not surprised.

I chose my accountant because his desk is almost as messy as mine, my car mechanic because I wasn't embarrassed to have him see the inside of my car. I've seen the inside of his.

I know that, like me, most messy people have remarkably organized minds. They have to — in order to keep track of their remarkably disorganized mess.

Better Late Forever

LAST FRIDAY, I REALIZED WITH SHOCK that the next day was my birthday. And with it came another annual headache: My Quebec driver's license would expire.

True, I had received the renewal form in the mail, four months earier, with a return envelope. But it was buried under a pile of dusty envelopes for my long-overdue phone bill, my unpaid property tax, and my expired passport.

I rushed downtown to the license bureau and spent the day in a lineup that got me to the wicket only moments before closing. It was a panicky, nerve-wracking, last-minute experience — like everything in my life.

Recently I confessed that I am a Type B Messy, whose office looks like it has been ransacked by burglars. But the truth is I am also a Type 2 Late, a congenital latecomer who never arrives anywhere until he is supposed to be somewhere else.

I am a member of life's Last-Minute Club. Many of you are probably unfortunate enough to know other members:

●They do not know it's Garbage Day until they hear the sound of the garbage truck. Then they chase after it with their Glad Bags, trailing orange peels and coffee grinds behind them.

●They never fill their gas tank until the fuel gauge has sunk to the bottom of the red zone. They only notice this when they are out on a remote highway at night, and must search for a 24-hour gas station, preserving fuel by coasting down hills in neutral.

(If they come upon a gas station, they do not have any cash, because their bank closed just before they got to it. And their bank card just expired).

●At movies, they always sit alone, even if they are with friends. By the time Type 2 arrives, there are only single seats left. In short, if life was a hockey game, they would only play in overtime.

My own career as a Type 2 started in grade school. Long before I had heard of Albert Einstein I knew that time was relative — to the number of things you had to cram into it.

I showed up for class promptly at 9:10 a.m. — 15 minutes after everyone else was in their seat. And like many latecomers, I learned to give creative excuses that were not quite a lie.

"I'm sorry, Miss. The bus stalled and there was this terrible traffic jam. Honest, Miss!"

Why mention that I was walking?

As an adult, I soon discovered a whole world of timetables waiting to be missed. For instance, the only time I catch a train is when I miss the one before it.

At airports, I am the guy running down the corridor while you stroll for coffee. In Lisbon, I once chased my charter flight down the runway.

Punctual people reading about my problem are probably convinced they can solve it — by buying me an agenda. In fact, some of you have already jotted it down in your own agenda:

"Send writer/wretch agenda for b.day."

Thanks, but spare yourself the trouble. I've received all kinds of agendas from punctual people determined to cure me — but it's hopeless. Agendas only make the organized more orderly and the punctual more prompt. They are utterly useless to the rest of us.

When a disorganized person gets an agenda, it is just one more responsibility to cope with. You have to mark things down and look things up, remember where the agenda is and switch it from one shirt pocket to the next. It's just another thing to make you late.

If I know a lot about latecomers, it's partly because I've met most of them, at least here in Montreal. Until a few years ago, all Quebec license plates expired on exactly the same day of the year — March 31, I believe.

I'll never forget the first time I showed up at the license bureau on that date. The lineup curled twice around the block, several thousand people standing in the cold, all clutching their expired licenses.

It was a kind of Festival of Lateness: a sorry collection of dalliers, dawdlers, lingerers, laggards, procrastinators, excuse-makers and other assorted latecomers — all eager to exchange exploits.

The man beside me never remembered to pay his Hydro bills until his lights went out. The woman next to him had a broken heel she'd meant to get fixed for two months.

Another fellow always paid his parking tickets — the minute the bailiff showed up at the door. He kept rushing away from the line to make sure his car wasn't being towed away.

There were no agendas to be seen in the crowd, but many people had fat wallets, stuffed like sausages with important scraps of papers they kept meaning to file. Many also had mismatched socks and rumpled shirts — because they hadn't gotten round to doing their laundry.

The friendships I made that day lasted years, because I met the same people in line on the same date every year, an annual convention of latecomers reunited happily by the provincial license bureau.

But several years ago, the bureaucrats suddenly changed the system and gave each driver an individual expiry date for their license. Sadly, the Festival of Latecomers was disbanded and we all scattered our own ways to our own delays.

I've often wondered what happened to my fellow latecomers. I search for their faces outside theatres, when I arrive 15 minutes late. I look for them at the central Post Office, at midnight, April 30, when I mail off my taxes.

But I have probably arrived too early, or too late. Who knows?

So if any of you are out there reading this, drop me a line in a month, or two, or whenever you get round to it. I'd love to hear from you.

Meanwhile, I'd better go. My editor just called from the paper to say this story is late.

The Gull War

III. VICTORY AT BALCONY

HI, MY NAME IS JOSH and I no longer have a pigeon problem.

Several weeks ago I described my battle with a nasty gang of delinquent pigeons, led by a fat, white bird named Attila. My story touched a nerve.

Since then, my telephone-answering machine has become a kind of pigeon hotline for people with their own stories — Pigeons Anonymous — leaving messages like:

"Hi, Mr. Freed. My name is Kathy, I'm 22 and I have a pigeon problem. Can you help me?"

I've received letters from Toronto, New York and even London, England, where a Mr. Nyett reports: "I have been under aerial bombardment for 20 years."

I got a letter from Keith, a computer nerd who spends his nights searching the Internet for a "Pigeon.die.die.die" discussion group.

This week I received a tip from a Chicago reader about a new anti-pigeon device sold there — a balloon with holographic owl eyes, called Terror-Eyes.

Many readers have suggested I leave out bird feed, spiked with birth-control pills. Apparently this wipes out future generations of pigeons and eventually solves the problem. Unfortunately, pigeons live about 35 years, so only my grandchildren will benefit.

Thank you for all your suggestions, but I no longer need assistance. I have dealt with my pigeons in my own way. No, do not be alarmed Ms. F., who wrote in huge letters:

"ARE YOU MURDERING PIGEONS, OR WHAT?"

I am not. Here is my last dispatch from the pigeon front:

When I last left off, my brother, Mike, was at the house preparing our final assault. He had already spent a week wrapping my balcony in thin piano wire, but the pigeons had fought their way through, snapping so many wires my balcony looked like a scene from *Escape from Alcatraz*.

He had also coated the balcony in a vat of Vaseline, a clever trick suggested by a reader who guaranteed it would work. It didn't. In fact, just after I finished writing my last pigeon report, I discovered Attila squatting in the far corner of the balcony with his pal Genghis.

I rushed outside and swung a broom at them but Attila stubbornly held his ground. I swung again and almost killed myself when I slipped on the Vaseline.

The commotion frightened off Attila, and I saw why he had been so stubborn. Attila had been sitting on an egg. "He" was a girl — Attila the Hen.

I disposed of the egg, and next morning my brother launched the final campaign of the Gull War. I had been advised by the city's leading anti-pigeon expert, the man who calls himself "Monsieur Pigeon."

"The most important thing is to get rid of the pigeon poop," he said. "Get rid of the scent and half the battle is over."

Pigeons were so stupid they would forget where they lived.

We rented an industrial cleaner, a huge noisy thing that blasted through the Vaseline and removed all trace of pigeon poop. Then, we tacked up 1,500 square feet of black netting that we draped over the building's balconies like a shroud. Finally, we coated the whole roof in a sticky glue that stings pigeons' feet.

The operation took three days and cost hundreds of dollars, but when it was over my building was pigeon-proofed. Unable to penetrate our defence, the enemy fled across the back courtyard to a neighbor's roof, like French invaders retreating across the British Channel.

All next day, Attila and his horde gathered on the roof, shrieking and cooing at the net — a grand council of pigeons deciding whether to declare war. We held our ground and waited.

But as the hours passed I could see their agitation diminish, as their limited memory bank was quickly erased. Within a day, they looked vacantly my way, with only a dim look of recognition — like pigeons experiencing déjà vu.

I imagined their conversation:

Attila: Hey, Genghis? See that weird building over there with the net? I could swear I've seen it somewhere before.

Genghis: Nahhh, it's probably just your imagination. Forget it.

Attila: I dunno. . . . And who's that weird bald guy sitting out on on a chair looking at us and laughing? Where did he come from?
Then again, who am I? Where did I come from?

In the weeks that followed, the flock began to break up into roving gangs, like chunks of the U.S.S.R. going their own way. Genghis and one group left first, and eventually Attila and the rest followed. By Moving Day — my pigeons had moved.

I admit that having my house shrouded in black net is not my favorite decor, but like the pigeon, we humans are an adaptive species. And it beats the alternative.

Neighbors down the block are complaining about a growing pigeon problem in their courtyards. One man reports that a fat, white bird keeps showing up on his balcony.

"It's very aggressive," he said. "What should I do?"

"Hmmm," I said. "I think I have some stories for you to read."

PRINTED BY
IMPRIMERIE D'ÉDITION MARQUIS
IN MAY 1996
MONTMAGNY (QUÉBEC)